Betty Pulkingham takes us on a humor‹ journey from her idyllic childhood ir marriage to a remarkable man, their yeaı the development of her international music career. Told with humor, joy, compassion, and mercy, this is a book well worth reading.

> Patricia Sprinkle,
> Author of *Friday's Daughter* and other novels.

Betty Carr Pulkingham's memoir reads like a novel—vivid, engaging, funny, wise. Few memoirists witness such unexpected, sustained, charismatic outpourings of the Holy Spirit. She did, and her response was to compose widely-sung music in testimony to miracles she observed. A gripping, tragic, victorious, comical, and deeply spiritual story.

> William Bradley Roberts
> Professor of Church Music
> Virginia Theological Seminary (Episcopal)

Betty Pulkingham tells her own story with disarming candor and a loving heart. The truth about her own life, including her marriage to a powerful, charismatic young Episcopal priest and how they, with a small band of lay people, opened their hearts and their homes to discouraged and marginalized people in a decaying inner city congregation, and how God lighted a fire of faith, hope and a new sound of music that the wind of the Spirit was to breathe across the world. This was part of a major breakthrough of spiritual renewal that permeated the entire church. Now millions of people sing songs and musical settings (for the Lord's Prayer and other parts of the Liturgy) that Betty and her musical companions wrote during those creative years.

She tells the story of the tragic turn of events that changed forever that meteoric trip across the sky, traces of which can still be seen and heard by those who look up in the night. A surprise read that touched me deeply.

> Keith Miller
> Author of the *Taste of New Wine*
> and *A Hunger for Healing*

This is my Story
This is my Song

A Life Journey

BETTY PULKINGHAM

WestBow
PRESS

Copyright © 2011 Betty Pulkingham

All rights reserved. No part of this book may be used or reproduced by any means, graphic, electronic, or mechanical, including photocopying, recording, taping or by any information storage retrieval system without the written permission of the publisher except in the case of brief quotations embodied in critical articles and reviews.

WestBow Press books may be ordered through booksellers or by contacting:

WestBow Press
A Division of Thomas Nelson
1663 Liberty Drive
Bloomington, IN 47403
www.westbowpress.com
1-(866) 928-1240

Because of the dynamic nature of the Internet, any web addresses or links contained in this book may have changed since publication and may no longer be valid. The views expressed in this work are solely those of the author and do not necessarily reflect the views of the publisher, and the publisher hereby disclaims any responsibility for them.

Any people depicted in stock imagery provided by Thinkstock are models, and such images are being used for illustrative purposes only.

Certain stock imagery © Thinkstock.

ISBN: 978-1-4497-2340-8 (e)
ISBN: 978-1-4497-2339-2 (sc)

Library of Congress Control Number: 2011914071

Printed in the United States of America

WestBow Press rev. date: 9/27/2011

To view Anthems, Mass Settings, and Recordings that feature Betty Pulkingham's compositions, go to www.communityofcelebration.com, click 'Enter our Secure Store,' type 'Betty Pulkingham' in the Search Box at the top of the page, and click 'Search.'

Contents

About the Cover vii
Acknowledgments 1
One: Lone Ranger 3
Two: A Goodly Heritage 10
Three: Bey And Leo 17
Four: Tarpley Street 25
Five: Dance, Sing And Play 31
Six: A Tarheel Bred 37
Seven: The Handsome Canadian 41
Eight: Matrimony 101 52
Nine: The Road Ahead 63
Ten: Motherhood 72
Eleven: Transitions 92
Twelve: My Life Goes . . . Tilt! 104
Thirteen: Music Wherever She Goes 113
Fourteen: A Journey Of The Heart 124
Fifteen: Across The Waters 132
Sixteen: A Larger Place 143
Seventeen: Another Land 156
Eighteen: To The Ends Of The Earth 167
Nineteen: Home Again 177
Twenty: Troubling Clouds 186
Twenty-one: Going Home 196
Twenty-two: Life With Bey And Jane 203
Twenty-three: The Road Curves 212
Twenty-four: Life Moves On 226

To the Fisherfolk, who traversed the world,
gladdening the hearts of God's people.
Their songs are with us even yet . . .

About the Cover

The famous mural known as *Christ of the Working Man* was painted by John William Orth in 1952. From that time until 2011 it hung as the reredos above the altar of Church of the Redeemer in Houston, Texas. The mural features many of the church members' images at the time of the painting. Marking the day of the final service in this building, the photograph was taken on Sunday, February 27, 2011.

Acknowledgments

It takes a village to raise a child. It has certainly taken a village to write this book. I am freshly aware of the many lives that have touched mine, the many people who have lent me their ears, their hearts, their skills as I went about this work.

    First on my list must be Keith Miller, friend and author, who has encouraged, challenged, prodded me on to "get 'er done" for several years. Even before that and some years ago, my soul-friend Benedict Reid had asked me, "Who is going to write the story of all that started at Redeemer?" While I was pretty sure that wouldn't be me, I was also not freed of the question and its significance. *Who would dare?* Who, in their right mind, could undertake to describe so many stories, so many lives, so much spiritual energy in play? Surely not me. But the question would not leave me. In the end, after taping several interviews with friends who had been involved in the movement, I decided there were just too many stories to be told, and I could only—in truth—tell my own, hoping that others would go and do likewise. So I have written a memoir.

    Many thanks go to Phil Bradshaw, Church of England priest and life-vowed member of the *Community of Celebration*, who wrote *Following the Spirit.* His book chronicles our shared history beginning in the early 1970's in England, when *Celebration* first came into being, and also gives theological insights as to the meaning of it all. Knowing his book was in the works released me from any pressure to become a community historian, something I felt ill-equipped to be.

Much credit goes to another author/friend, Patricia Sprinkle, for being my first reader and offering great help as editor and consultant. When first asked if she were willing to help me, she said, "Yes. I've been waiting for this book for years!"

My faithful reader and fact-checker and longtime companion in the Way has been Bill Farra from *Celebration*. He was indispensable in supplying dates when things happened, and oftimes specifics of *what* happened in areas where my memories were vague. His winsome spirit and hearty laughter always put fresh wind in my sails. Daphne Grimes, Episcopal priest and friend of many years, had an ear to hear and a heart to encourage me; Carl Daw offered sage counsel as I pursued publication; and the faithful intercessions of Patricia Allen for my entire family have undergirded all that I do.

To those who offered me technical assistance along the way: to Michelle Farra, to Ben Ansbacher, to Sandra Briggs—for their computer skills where mine fell far short; to Mimi Farra who provided indispensable copyright information; to diligent proofreaders Joe Beckey and Kathy Hykes; to Virginia Paget who shared her home, her good cooking, and her computer with me on my visits to Texas: please know I could never have done it without you.

Finally, to all my praying friends who wanted me to write this book: to Rose Anne Gant who read the very first chapter before there *were* any more chapters; to Cattie McCormick who has loved me through all the ups and downs of my life; to Betsey Savage who brightened my path and gave me hope in difficult spots; and to my longtime faithful shepherd David Williams; my gratitude knows no bounds. To God be the glory.

Betty Carr Pulkingham

One
Lone Ranger

How on earth did a nice conservative girl like me from central North Carolina end up in Houston's decaying East End? Here I was, in a church so dim I could scarcely read the printed order of service before me. My husband Graham was ascending the pulpit to preach his first sermon at Church of the Redeemer. Had the Spirit of God literally *driven* me into the Texas wilderness to meet my destiny? It was beginning to feel that way as I looked back.

August 1949 . . . "All aboard!" The conductor's cry ricocheted down the tracks. My parents were waving from the platform. Steam rose between us lending an impressionistic aura to the moment. *Unforgettable.* Slowly . . . ever so slowly the Southerner eased away from the depot as if knowing I needed a lingering moment to absorb it all. Then gaining speed, it was off on its long, long journey south to New Orleans. I had just turned twenty-one and my odyssey had begun.

Maybe it began even earlier when I spent my first summer after college heading north to do graduate work in music. I knew I was out of my native habitat when I asked a cab driver in Rochester, New York if he could *carry* me to the Eastman School of Music. He roared with laughter and said, "Well, I guess I *could.*" Hard to imagine that six weeks of graduate study would land me my first job at a university clear across country.

Maybe my odyssey began even earlier, when my mother became my advocate for studying music in the first place—a profession my daddy described as extremely *non-lucrative*.

At any rate, here I was with plenty of time to think the matter over. The wheels were rolling and would hopefully roll all the way into New Orleans. There I would change trains for the westward leg of the trip, Southern Pacific *carrying* me, God willing, to Austin, Texas. After the sorting and packing of past weeks, how nice to let my soul lie fallow for awhile and process some feelings. This was my first night in a Pullman berth. I was grateful for a lower berth so I didn't have to reveal my ineptitude by clambering up to God knows where. It was a good night and I think you could call it sleep—that gentle jostling back and forth and occasional clicks on the tracks beneath, altogether a lulling sensation begetting drowsiness.

"Hello, Hilda!" It was early morning in New Orleans as I greeted an old friend from Carolina. She and her Tulane professor/husband, came to meet the train and show me around the French quarter—a delightful break in the long journey. Now it reminds me how my past was prologue to an about-to-unfold future. Hilda had once been Director of Religious Education at the Methodist church in Burlington where I grew up. She was one of those who had encouraged me in studying music. A matronly, plain person with a heart of gold, she would sometimes meet me at the church after school and we would enjoy music together. She would play the piano and I would sing songs like *Carry Me Back to old Virginy* and *Londondery Air*. Songs like that. At the threshold of my teen years Hilda had offered me a musical outlet for feelings. What a gift. So, yes, my past was clearly traveling with me; God had some special angels assigned to my case.

The plains of east Texas stretched out before me as the train snaked its way towards Houston. Eventually I got tired counting cows, though I could still recall the childhood pleasure of cow poker in the back seat with my younger brother Jim as sole competitor. It was more fun then—just too many cows here. There was, however, a more immediate parlor game going on, as I seemed to have attracted the attention of a forty-ish man who kept asking me questions—especially about where I was getting off the train. He even asked me to stop over in Houston so he could show me around. Nice fellow, I guess, but far too pushy. *Is this what it means to be propositioned?* It felt uncomfortable. I tried changing the subject several times, then engrossed myself in a book I had brought along to read, hoping that maybe, just maybe he would get discouraged. Finally, he did. Thank goodness.

So this is Texas. The Chamber of Commerce didn't know I was coming, did they? As we pulled into the Southern Pacific station in Austin there stood a guy topped with an enormous ten-gallon hat and shod with glistening leather cowboy boots. Tall and lanky—I'd say six foot eight or so, he was very handsome. My eyes lit on him before I stepped off the train, and what can I say? I knew I was in Texas. Later I would learn that he was a graduate music student at U.T., part of a German settler-family the likes of which were prevalent in that part of the world. Seeing him now convinced me: *this is the place I've been longing to see. I took the right train. This is where my new life begins.*

My little cubby-hole of a room in Miss Dot Thornton's house was a place you could hide and never be found. Maybe that's why I chose it; my unspoken fears were beginning to surface. Miss Dot was an elderly spinster living in the University neighborhood within an easy walk to the music building. It was a quiet neighborhood, safe and tucked away from the madding world. Here I could unpack, settle in and prepare myself for the challenges ahead. I was the only roomer in the house, the rent was reasonable, she was a pleasant and unassuming landlady, so all was good.

Miss Dot had some interesting friends, one of whom was Miss Ima Hogg, noted patron of the arts from Houston and daughter of the late Texas Governor, legend having it that he had named his other daughter "Ura." Such tales convinced me there was a brand of Texas humor from which I had been mercifully protected until now. One interesting historical note: the Thornton family hailed from Virginia, and Miss Dot was a direct descendant of Patrick Henry. When I came in at night, I walked straight past a chest that had belonged to old *"Give me liberty . . . "* himself. That should keep me minding my p's and q's.

This proved a useful reminder as I began to move about and meet people. Being barely twenty-one and having tall blond credentials seemed to attract certain "on-the-make" men, who liked to take me out and buy me drinks. Before my social life had blossomed very far, however, I turned my attention to getting down to business: suiting up and showing up at the University of Texas, where I had contracted to be an Instructor in Music Theory in the School of Fine Arts.

Having unpacked, I surveyed the neighborhood for places to eat. The Night Hawk was my favorite, and fortuitously right on my walking route to U.T. One fine morning I decided, *this is the day I go turn myself in at the Music Building*—easier said than done, as it turns out. Fortified with a good Night Hawk breakfast and wearing presentable clothing, I marched right down Guadalupe, known to university natives as "the drag," and took a right on 21st Street. A short ways down, just this side of the impressive U.T. fountain with mustangs and leaping water-spouts, *there it was.* On my left in full view was the Music Building. That's where I was headed.

There was just one small problem: *My feet won't take me there; what is wrong with my feet?* Well, it would be good to walk around the block, get a feel for the neighborhood. So I acquiesced to my feet and walked around the block—several times. Each time I came back to the front of that building something inside said, *Not yet.* So, I walked around again. Was I waiting for number seven? Hoping the walls would come tumbling down? Oh, help!

Until that moment, truth to tell, I had not faced into my fears, thinking they would go away on their own. But there they were in full array and in complete agreement with my feet, of whom they seemed to be master at the moment. *Why am I so terrified?* OK, I needed to be completely rational for a minute here: I had never been this far away from home, number one. Number two: I had never even been west of the Mississippi before. Number three: I didn't know a soul here, save the dean who hired me, and I certainly didn't know him well; if he knew how I was feeling at the moment he might regret his rash decision back in Rochester. Number four: I was to join a faculty of much more experienced and seasoned professionals. The ink on my college diploma was barely dry and here I was—about to meet some very distinguished artists and teachers who had been "doing their thing" for years. *No wonder I am scared to death.*

It would be many years before deeper insights emerged about this psychological crisis in my life: about my womanhood and the societal expectations of that day. Where I grew up in the South, women weren't *supposed* to leave home and blaze new trails. "Go west, young woman" was not an imperative; it was young men who were supposed to be the adventurers. Young women were supposed to learn to be ladylike in their demeanor, and prepare themselves to be dutiful mothers and homemakers, and oh yes, choose a college major which would serve them well until the right man came along. So, what I had done flew in the face of what I had been raised to do.

Yet the motto of my high school class had been "Hitch your wagon to a star." Girls and boys alike had been encouraged to dream and hope, to think big thoughts and defy a few expectations; and my college years at Woman's College of the University of North Carolina had been a terrific laboratory for developing leadership skills. There were no men around to compete with or be distracted by. In this environment young women flourished academically and discovered and developed their own gifts, free from pressure of relating to the opposite sex—at least until the weekends rolled 'round.

After several walks around the block, my feet gave in to my carefully reasoned insistence that going into the Music Building was the *only* thing to do. I would just have to grasp the nettle, endure the pain, and hope for relief from my *angst* by doing the very thing I dreaded most: "turning myself in." Hiding any longer was not an option. So, in I went.

Dean William Doty welcomed me cordially, even warmly. *Thank God he remembers me.* He told me things I needed to know about the set-up, and reminded me that there would be another new Instructor named Shirley Lewis—*am I ever eager to meet her—another freshman instructor, green as I am.* He took me to the Music Theory office, introduced me to the head instructor, then left.

Miss Herdwood was a thirty-ish woman with brown bobbed hair, dark horned-rim glasses and a brusque, business-like manner. She was not southern—at least not from the land of magnolias and soft-spoken cadences familiar to me. She showed me my desk, told me what was expected of me, and then we went home. I was glad: glad my feet had brought me here, glad to see the nice dean again, glad the suspense was over and I could draw a deep breath. *Whew.*

I found my way home again by way of the *Night Hawk* where I discovered a delicious fruit salad topped with pink creamy dressing—a nice lite-bite for supper, and only thirty-five cents. In the weeks and months ahead I would enjoy many more of these, occasionally treating myself to one of their famous Frisco burgers, too. One good thing about having to walk everywhere was that *you did just that* without giving it a second thought. Fifteen or twenty years later I would have been considered disadvantaged without a car, but I was blissfully unaware of that at the moment and all the healthier for it.

As the days went by I met other people in the Music Department. One of the most interesting was Kent Kennan, resident composer and teacher of composition and orchestration. An older bachelor, he was clearly not the marrying type or it would already have happened. So he was a "safe" male friend for me, and ever so kind. I discovered his older brother was the distinguished George Kennan of diplomatic fame. Kent took me to Green Pastures, a wonderful home-cum-restaurant some miles outside of Austin in a lovely rural setting. The cream of asparagus soup was superb. So was the setting of the old house, with its gracious grounds. Going there was a real outing. Today, of course, Green Pastures has been subsumed in south Austin, minutes away from overcrowded loops and highways. So we have pastures no longer, only progress now, if you can find it in your heart to call it that.

Finally I met Shirley, the other "freshman" instructor. We hit it off right away. She was short and brunette, I was tall and blond; she German and methodical, I Anglo-Saxon and intuitive. We both loved music and were searching for a church connection here. We would have lots of good times together. She was especially eager to try out the Mexican restaurants, and so was I. We enjoyed eating outside on the patios in the relative cool of the evening. It never turned *really* cool here until winter. She put generous amounts of hot sauce on her already spicy tacos, then needed considerable cooling off—with waiters scurrying to bring butter to put on her tongue and many glasses of ice water, while I dived into my purse for extra handkerchiefs to wipe her tear-ing eyes. It was quite an adventure going out to eat Mexican food with Shirley, who repeated the aforementioned behavior with maddening regularity.

So, the first stage of my odyssey had begun. I was here. I was safe and sound. I was an employed musician. I was getting to know people. I was even beginning to feel somewhat at home at my work space in the Music Theory office, though totally unaware that it was in this very space that I would meet my future husband a year hence. Occasionally I had to ask myself: *How on earth did I get here?* How did I have the courage to become a Lone Ranger venturing deep into the heart of Texas? It was really only a fleeting thought. It would be years before I looked back and gave full credit to God's Spirit, that Spirit who is loose in the world, leading and guiding those who put their trust in a relationship with the Divine Other.

> *If I take the wings of the morning*
> *and dwell in the uttermost parts of the sea,*
> *Even there your hand will lead me*
> *and your right hand hold me fast.*
> *Psalm 139: 8-9* [1]

---

[1] Psalm verses throughout are from the *Book of Common Prayer,* 1979.

Two
A Goodly Heritage

We all come from somewhere, and North Carolina is as good a place as you could choose if the choosing were up to you. Surely my roots in the Old North State had prepared me for launching out into the wild west, though there was little time to ruminate on that at the moment. Instead, I focused on what was new and challenging and right in front of my face. As it turns out, North Carolina is a good place to come home to as well—something we will get to later.

My parental roots go back deeply into North Carolina's history, the paternal side from solid Scots-Irish farming stock who settled in the flatlands of eastern Carolina. My grandparents' home was a modest small farmhouse in Duplin County. On visits my only sleeping space was a little room just off the sitting room, where I would fall asleep to the lulling sound of male voices—my grandfather, daddy and his four brothers spinning yarns and sharing jokes, punctuated by resonant chuckles. Occasionally they would sing a hymn together, led by Uncle Carlisle with his rich bass voice. The memory is one of such warmth and security—as though I were being cradled, rocked in a soft blanket of love.

My grandfather, Calvin Johnson Carr, was a prince of a man, tall and strong, with a beautiful shock of snow-white hair and a heavy mustache. Going to visit him in Duplin County was a serious trek over partially unpaved roads; it was sure to be dark when we arrived. He would throw his head back as he greeted us with a hearty laugh saying, "Well! I was so worried about you I fell fast asleep." This was a little indication of the enormous reservoir of faith he possessed. He was not one to worry; he was one to trust the Lord. He had become a lay-preacher and well-known circuit rider in later years, the only one of my relatives who knew about Azusa Street, the site of the early twentieth century Pentecostal revival, and who practiced glossalalia. This made him a little suspect amongst some of the family members, who thought he had "gone off the deep end" with religion. Of course, I was unaware of any of this as a child, but simply remember him as a big, bold preacher-man with a big welcoming presence.

His wife, my paternal grandmother, had died when my daddy was only five years old. That must have been so hard for him, as the oldest of three very young children she left behind. He and his sisters were raised substantially by their grandparents. Meanwhile my grandfather remarried and had seven children by his second wife. For farm families around the turn of the century having a big family was no luxury but a practical necessity—in order to work the fields, harvest the crops, feed the chickens and milk the cows. It is not surprising that I never got to know my step-grandmother well; she was a busy lady, with a busy life and lots of grandkids besides. But *Ma-ma* was another story.

My mother's mother, Betty Frances Buchanan—*Ma-ma* to us all—was a memorable woman. She married Samuel Waite Knott, the third of twenty children born to Fielding R. Knott, a successful landowner in Granville County. It had taken him two wives to accomplish this feat—not the landowning part, but the twenty children. His success impresses me in two ways, one of them material, the other moral. First of all, he was able to leave each of his twenty children a farm, with a house; that seems remarkable to me. Secondly, he never owned any slaves: never wanted to, perhaps never *needed* to given his large number of children.

Ma-ma's family came from Clan Buchanan in Scotland, numbering many artists and teachers. The first, James Buchanan, came to America in 1617. The Knotts and Buchanans settled near Oxford in the center of the state. Some of my earliest and dearest memories go back along those country roads, or meandering through the large grove of handsome oak trees surrounding *Ma-ma's* and *Pa-pa's* home outside of Oxford. As a young girl playing *house* amongst the huge oak roots, I organized each space into a different room. My favorite space to sleep was an upstairs feather bed, my favorite slumbering time a rainy day when raindrop magic was playing on the tin roof overhead. The Oxford house was an altogether wonderful place for a child to be and recall. I always cried when we had to leave. All the way home I cried—for sixty miles: *that's* how much I didn't want to leave. Small wonder: it was a place where family gathered, a richer environment than my ordinary life as an only child. But home I went, until the next gathering or funeral, whichever came first.

When I was five-and-a-half *Pa-pa* died. Standing beside my cousin Betsy at his funeral, we noticed many of the grown-ups dabbing their eyes with handkerchiefs. We decided to cry also—apparently the acceptable mode of behavior at a funeral. Pa-pa would have found that amusing. He was a fun-loving guy, *Sam* to his nine children, who just had too much fun with him to call him a serious name like *father*.

Ma-ma's forebears were just as interesting as Sam's. Her father, John Ruffin Buchanan, was a skilled woods-craftsman who used to do hand-tooled decorative work, *banji-work*, on the exterior of Victorian mansions. He also crafted beautiful furniture. He fought for the Confederacy in the Civil War, and was seriously wounded at the Battle of South Anna River in 1863. Given up for dead but spared the final sword-thrust rendered many wounded and dying soldiers to shorten their suffering, he was brought to a Confederate hospital in Richmond. When my great-grandmother Nancy heard he had been taken there, she drove a horse and buggy all the way from Oxford to Richmond to find him.

"You are too late," she was told. "The death wagon has come to take him away." She insisted on seeing him for herself. A white sheet had been placed over him but she raised it, leaned close to him, touched his hand and called his name several times. His eyes flickered open. He was alive—barely. She stayed by his side as his nurse until he was strong enough to make the trip back home to Carolina. One of his lungs had been shot out, but that did not prevent his returning to his woodworking craft after he had regained strength. Carrying his tool kit, he would walk to neighboring towns where he had been hired to do work. Neighbors passing him in their buggies offered him a ride, to which he replied cheerily, "No thanks, not today. I'm in a hurry." I reckon that these walks provided just the kind of aerobic exercise he needed to stay healthy. He lived until the ripe old age of eighty-seven.

His daughter Betty Frances was both dutiful and devoted. As was the norm in those days, older relations lived alongside the younger working ones who kept an eye on them in their dotage. So it was that my great-grandfather used to wander off at times. The truth is that even after his wood-working years were over he still loved walking. When this happened, Betty Frances would send one of the girls out to tell him to come home. My aunt Jane could remember running after him as a small child, calling,

"Grandpa! Grandpa, Ma-ma says come *back*." At first he would not heed her call, but after several desperate cries he would turn around and train his steely blue eyes on her and say, 'Well, if Betty Frances says to come back, I'll *come* back. *But*— I'm not taking orders from any little old whipper-snapper."

Ma-ma was a good mother, a stern disciplinarian—she left the having fun part to Sam—and a woman of a serious religious disposition. From their earliest years, my mother and aunts remembered trekking to church with *Ma-ma*, who played the piano and led the singing at their little Knotts' Grove Baptist Church. Discipline was never an issue even when they were small. One lifted eyebrow from *Ma-ma* was all it took to restore perfect order on the front row where the children were seated. She frequently took the girls with her to visit neighboring churches. They were part of her "Sunbeam" group, her sample *beams*, my mother used to say. These were the beams of the famous Baptist chorus: "Jesus wants me for a sunbeam."

Not only did *Ma-ma* have musical gifts, she also had medical ones. She was a natural-born healer to whom all neighbors turned in time of need. She functioned much as a nurse practitioner does today. Possessing a volume called Gunn's *Newest Family Physician and Home Book of Health*, published in 1875, she would consult it as needed to help in a health crisis. The whole Knotts Grove community knew to consult "Aunt Betty" first; only if *she* said so would they call for the doctor. She became an expert in detecting the effects of a hangover, and a staunch believer in a reliable spring tonic for children: castor oil. *Oh, my.* I still recall that awful, oily mess down your throat, followed by a chaser of orange juice. It's enough to turn you off orange juice for life.

By the time I joined the inevitable castor-oil-for-kids club, Ma-ma was in her seventies and no longer applying the spring tonic herself. That job fell to her oldest son Ed. Mercifully, I have one positive memory of him to offset this: he gave me a hands-on lesson in how to milk a cow. I never quite got the hang of it—there was so much hanging down—but he was very patient and kind. His only daughter Mary Frances, quite a bit older than I, was my idol, my model; she was what I wanted to turn out to be. Mind you, I *had* other first cousins, but when someone referred to Betsy, or Marsha, or Ethel, as my first cousins, I would correct them firmly: "No. Mary Frances is my *first* cousin." Full-stop. No doubt about it. She *was* my first cousin. Others were second, or third; she alone wore the crown.

Surely my cousin Betsy would have come in second. Closer to my own age, we palled around at family gatherings, had our pictures taken at the old well on the farm, cried at funerals together, and were good cousin/friends. When I was twelve, I rode the train to Charlotte to visit her. What an adventure. It was my first train trip of any length, barring the time my parents had taken me with them to New York to the Worlds Fair in 1940. But this was *on my own*. We had a simply delicious time, judging

This is my Story This is my Song

from the fact that my one lingering memory is that of going to a downtown hotel for lunch and ordering—or did someone do it for me?—*coq-au-vin*. I had never tasted wine in my life, but what it did for that chicken was indescribable.

My mother had eight siblings—six brothers and two sisters. The rambling old farmhouse where *Ma-ma* and *Pa-pa* raised their nine children usually accommodated several others as well. Typically they were school teachers, or cousins who needed tending due to some family situation. Their extended family formed the nucleus of the Knotts' Grove community. The one and only elementary school in the area met in their house, and they were the founding family in the church across the road, which bore their name.

In her nineties "Bey," the nickname my mother acquired in later years, attended a family reunion in Granville County and was surprised when a local resident, also a nonagenarian, approached her and asked,

"Are you Betty Frances?" When she nodded yes, he gave her a big hug. "All my life I've wanted to meet you," he said. I remember the day you were born. We got a school holiday on account of you."

Not surprising, since the classes met upstairs in the house, just across the hall from the bedroom where the delivery took place. A few years later, when Bey was still a very young girl, she recalled the upstairs once again being off-limits—this time due to the critical illness of her older brother Pierce who had contracted typhoid fever. Nurses from Richmond had been hired to tend him round the clock, and the swish of their stiffly starched uniforms and the "Shhs . . ." of the adults shushing the other children were sounds Bey would never forget. Unfortunately Pierce succumbed to the dread disease, taking with him a marvelous musical talent which had motivated him to learn to play several instruments, including the violin.

Photos from the early 1900's, digitally restored and astounding in their clarity, show the family gathered outside the old farmhouse, each of the boys with a musical instrument in hand: guitar, mandolin, banjo, violin. They had their own family "band" for sure, and loved making music together. Bey wanted to learn the piano, but with older brothers away in college, it would have strained the family budget. It's the one complaint she *ever* expressed about her childhood. She regretted not being able to learn to play the piano. And years later? She made sure to provide me an excellent piano teacher when I turned eight. Now I realize how invested she was personally in the development of my musical gifts. Listening to *me* play the piano was for her a re-ignition of her own desires, cast in a vicarious framework and deeply satisfying.

Faith, family, farming, music: these were basic realities and values for my family of origin. How blessed I am to have known some of these people well, and to have known others through the stories that were passed down.

> *My boundaries enclose a pleasant land;*
> *indeed, I have a goodly heritage.*
> *Psalm 16: 6*

Three
Bey and Leo

Some marriages are designed in heaven, and this one surely was. My mother *Bey*, named Betty Frances for her mother, was born in November 1899, just before the turn of the century. My father, six years older, was named Leo—no middle name, just Leo. Combined with his surname 'Carr' that makes seven letters, a minimalist approach to the business of naming. The only nickname he ever had was "Box"—as in *box-car* from the great days of trains, I suppose.

As a boy Leo was fascinated with trains. In the small kitchen of his family's farmhouse there was a window where he sat for hours, sticking his head outside and waving to passers-by on the platform of his imaginary train. He was the engineer, of course. What could have fascinated a young land-locked boy more than imagining a trip to a faraway place on a train? You could go *anywhere.* As a youngster from a hard-working farmer's family who scarcely went anywhere their feet couldn't take them, Leo would find release through his imagination into the outside world of industry and science, commerce and fine institutions of learning, the world of the arts and all things beautiful. This was very likely the cradle of his thirst for knowledge and higher learning.

It didn't come easily, of course. He worked his way through The University of North Carolina by raising and marketing strawberries in his native Duplin County. He would attend college for a couple of semesters, then work to earn enough to return for more learning. After graduation, feeling a call to the legal profession, he worked his way through law school by taking a job as principal of a small school in his home county—again balancing academic studies with the business of holding down a job. It was in this latter capacity as principal that he met my mother one summer in Chapel Hill. She was there with her older sister Pearl, whom we all called *Sister*—I really think because her full name was Nanny Pearl, and no one who loved her could bring themselves to say it. My mother had just graduated *magna cum laude* from Oxford College in her hometown by the same name. The summer school session in Chapel Hill was her debut onto a larger landscape. She was undoubtedly *psyched* to explore her future as a qualified teacher.

One evening Bey and Pearl attended a play put on by the Carolina Players at UNC. For some reason Bey could not take her eyes off the young man playing the lead in this historical drama. Afterwards, back at the rooming house where they were staying, she told Sister,

"I would like to meet that young man." Pearl laughed out loud.

"*Meet* him? How are you going to meet him? Don't be absurd. You'll likely never see him again."

Bey carried on about it for awhile until Sister finally said, "I don't want to hear another word. *Just be quiet and go to sleep. Do you hear?*" So she did. The next morning, the housemother knocked on the door of their room.

"Is Betty Frances here?" Bey opened a crack in the door to the hallway as the housemother continued, "There's a young man downstairs to see you."

"Who is he?" asked Bey.

"He's the principal of a school down east," she replied.

"I'll be down shortly." Bey wondered who on earth this could be so early in the morning. She dressed and went downstairs, and . . . miracle of miracles, there was her hero. This was the same young man who had performed the previous evening, whom she had dreamed about last night. *How did he know about her? Had he read her mind? What was he doing here?* Her face felt flushed. But he set her at ease by smiling and saying,

"You are Miss Betty Frances Knott, I believe?" She extended her hand and nodded assent. "My name is Leo Carr. I am principal of a small school in Duplin County. I hope I haven't disturbed you too early. The thing is: someone gave me your name as an eligible teacher, and I am here to inquire if you would be interested in teaching in my school."

Well. There it was—the opportunity she had been looking for professionally, all wrapped up in an irresistible package. They talked. With appropriate restraint, she promised to let him know after she had had time to consider the offer.

Her first thought was, "I must talk to Miss Hobgood." Her college counselor and Latin teacher was someone Bey admired and whose judgment she trusted. On a special trip home to Oxford she wasted no time finding her beloved teacher. Flushed with excitement, she began pouring out her story about the extraordinary meeting with this young man, how he had found her and offered her a teacher's position in his school. Finally she stopped to catch her breath and it was Miss Hobgood's turn to speak. The wise old teacher was quiet for a minute, then spoke slowly, weighing her words well.

"Betty Frances," she said, "it sounds like a very interesting teaching position." She paused before going on. "There's just one thing I want to say to you about it." Bey was on the edge of her seat listening.

"Don't agree to teach in this young man's school unless you intend to marry him."

Bey's mouth fell open. "*Marry* him? Miss Hobgood, I have *no* such thought in my mind. I just can't believe you *said* that." She was indignant.

"Because," her teacher carried on, "there is one thing I know to be true, my dear. Marriage is a matter of proximity."

A matter of proximity . . . hmm. Bey tried to let the words of her beloved teacher sink in, but inside a raging battle was going on. Had she not just achieved the long-sought-after college degree which none of the previous generation of women in her family had? Had she not put her name on a list of qualified teachers, to which this young principal had responded? Was this not what professional people did? Was this not how they behaved? Had she not been approached purely and simply because of those qualifications? Where did the idea of marriage come into the picture anyway? All of the smoldering indignation of hitherto unexpressed "women's lib" feelings welled up. It wasn't fair. Why couldn't a woman work hard, gain her qualifications, apply for and accept a job—without strings attached?

Years later Bey would look back and recall this moment and her teacher fondly, acknowledging that there was experience borne of living behind those words. But for now? She was determined that marriage had nothing to do with it. To prove it, she did not go out on a date with my father for a full year after he had employed her as a teacher.

Not only that—she left no stone unturned in exploring that deep sense of God's calling upon her life which had been with her since age seventeen. Her earliest childhood memories were of songs her mother sang to her about the love of Jesus. She had accepted Jesus Christ as her Savior at age ten, but it was when she was seventeen that the Lord sealed the deal. While at Oxford College she was attending a service of worship one night when a hymn of dedication was announced. As everyone was singing *Have Thine Own Way, Lord*, these lines somehow leapt off the page and into her spirit:

> *Mold me and shape me, 'til all shall see*
> *Christ only, always, living in me.*

At that moment and in that very place she asked the Lord to take her life and make that a reality: that He would live his life through her. It was as though Jesus were speaking directly to her and to her alone. It was her moment of total surrender to the Lord whom she would serve all of her days. This baptism in

This is my Story This is my Song

the Spirit, as many would call it, this unequivocal surrender to Jesus Christ, would place everything and everyone else in her life in a secondary position.

Here's how she described it to a beloved grand-daughter who was contemplating marriage: "When Leo proposed marriage to me in 1921, the substance of my reply was 'only if you're willing to take second place in my life. Jesus Christ will always come first.' Being the great Christian that he was, he had no fault with that. We deferred our engagement; I went to Louisville, Kentucky to a theological seminary for a year—to study, to think, to walk closely with the Lord and be *sure* that He wasn't calling me in a different direction. We both dated other people. I didn't even see him for a year. We both prayed a lot, and honestly tried to let the Lord lead in our relationship."

My daddy's letters during this period reveal the depths of who *he* was, as well. In 1922 alone he wrote her 159 letters, and the grand total for their four-year courtship was 759—a staggering total by any of today's standards. Years later, upon her housekeeper's discovery of all these letters in the attic of her home, Bey wrote: "What a thrill to live again the excitement of age 20 at age 95. These precious letters have brought Judge Carr so vividly back to me that I often seem to hear his footsteps, the sound of his voice, and feel the warmth of his tender embrace. That he should have written with such bold and legible strokes, and always with a *good* fountain pen, has enabled my fast fading eyesight to enjoy reading them again after 75 years. I give God full credit for all of this. It is just another evidence of His incredible mercy and goodness. There is no language that can express my gratitude."

Letters say what e-mail messages rarely do, and Leo was able to convey much to his young sweetheart through these letters. As she still struggled to discern the Lord's calling on her life, he assured her that, much as it might grieve him, he would not stand in her way if she continued to feel called to be a missionary instead of marrying him. He did insert a short *commercial* of sorts in one letter, pointing out that through marriage and the raising of children a woman could in essence change the world.

Eventually they *were* married, but the self-imposed soul-searching process they went through speaks volumes to me. It always has. Their doing their homework prepared me for doing mine. Somehow they put me in the frame of mind that matrimony is *holy*. Either you are called by God—by a holy God—to a holy state of being called marriage; or you are not. Christ's first miracle at the marriage feast in Cana of Galilee says it all to me: Marriage is *itself* a miracle—when it works. When two people have faith enough to believe in impossible things, they just *might* make it through a marriage. Some marriages fail, and for understandable reasons. *But from the beginning it was not so* . . . That's how Jesus reminded his questioners about God's original, high, and holy purposes for marriage. Every Christian marriage needs this buoy, this vision, and the couple's own faith alive, even to get *started* down this road.

Their way was not easy—Bey and Leo's. Married in 1924, they began their life together in Burlington, where Leo had chosen to start his practice of law. Their first home was a boarding-house on Broad Street where they rented a room with boarding privileges. Hanging up your shingle as a new-in-town lawyer must be tough, even in good times. Leo had come to Burlington a year earlier and had a good feeling about the place. Bey recalls her first Sunday at First Baptist Church:

"Pastor Buck's wife was waiting for me just outside the door after the service. She *already* had a job in mind for me in the Sunday School." Bey's fame had traveled before her. Her credentials included numerous certificates and diplomas from the Southern Baptist Convention via their educational divisions, and a WMU Training Certificate for completing a one-year course at the seminary in Louisville. She was plunged forthwith into *church work* as they call it. I don't know who originated the term, but it is self-describing. All churches need workers, of the volunteer variety.

This was a very good thing since—to her amazement—*Bey* did not qualify as a school-teacher now that she had moved to Alamance County. Why? *She was now married.* The laws in Burlington forbade hiring a married school-teacher. Strange as that may seem to our 21st century ears, it was nonetheless the law of the time in the place where she lived. The likelihood of pregnancy and child-bearing would have complicated the employer's situation, I suppose. So there she was, without a house to "keep," and with lots of time on her hands. Thank God for church work.

Many of the friends she made were school teachers who had come to Burlington as single women, *then* married. The rule didn't apply to them; they kept their jobs. Aside from nursing, teaching was the only viable profession for women at the time. There were undoubtedly other college-educated women who fell into the same snare that Bey had and suffered disappointment. All I can say about that is that in Bey's case, the school system's loss was the church's great gain.

One way the gals—Bey and her young matron friends—kept their minds alive and questing was through a most timely thing called the "book club." The one *Bey* was invited to join was the Mentor Book Club. Meeting monthly in members' homes, light refreshments were served on fine bone china, and tea was generally poured from a silver tea service. Preceding this was the serious business of the club: A book or topic was studied, and a member who had steeped herself in the topic for months gave a report on her research, in the form of an interesting program. Sometimes a speaker from one of the prestigious universities nearby came to speak. Years later when I became a member of the Junior Mentor Book Club—which ridiculous title the club kept until some members were pushing eighty—I began to realize what a godsend this club had been in the mid-twenties. As secretary I pored through old books of minutes, read the description of programs given, and was dumbfounded by the scope and depth of the topics studied. I still recall the time when *Bey*, in her fifties then, read books and studied for months in preparation for giving a program on cartels.

Cartels, for heaven's sake. Today's women seem to need something much more frothy, and get their intellectual challenges elsewhere; but not then. This club was an intellectual lifeline for *Bey* and her friends.

Meanwhile, Leo was making his own way as an attorney-at-law. He had joined a firm with two other lawyers: *Coulter, Cooper, & Carr*, shortly after his arrival in Burlington, and had soon become involved in politics. Having served his country in the armed forces during World War I, he now served his county as chairman of the Democratic Executive Committee and as county attorney. Little could he have known that in less than ten years he would be appointed Judicial Solicitor for his district of the state of North Carolina, and that in 1938 he would be elected as Superior Court Judge of the Tenth Judicial District—a position he held unopposed by a candidate from either party—until his retirement in 1970. All of this was up ahead.

But for now? The two of them—*Bey* and Leo—had established themselves in a town they would never leave. They had come there to live, to serve, and hopefully if God willed, to raise a family. Theirs was a solid union of body, mind and spirit.

Happy are they all who fear the Lord,
    and who follow in his ways!
You shall eat the fruit of your labor;
    happiness and prosperity shall be yours.
Psalm 128: 1-4

Four
Tarpley Street

It was one block long—the block where we lived on Tarpley Street. At least it looked that way to the eyes of a child. Tarpley Street ran between Front and Davis. Years later I noticed that it meandered east of Front Street all the way to the railroad tracks. That was out of my orbit as a young girl; but the block I knew was a wonderful place, a safe place, a friendly neighborhood full of young families with kids. Front lawns were tiny, houses close together, and we played in the street quite safely. It was rare to see a car drive down Tarpley Street unless it belonged to someone who lived there. Our house was a green shingled bungalow, modest and substantial, where we lived until I was eight years old. On summer evenings at twilight the children used to gather outside, collecting fireflies in bottles as evening shadows deepened. Tarpley Street was a magical place for a child.

The anticipation of my birth in 1928 had meant that Bey and Leo needed a bigger place than the one room where they started their married life. A larger home had been in Leo's mind all along. In one of those famous 759 letters to Bey, he shared how he and a friend named Ralph Holt had discussed sharing a house on Tarpley Street, but had concluded their wives would probably not be happy sharing a kitchen with "another woman." Interestingly, Ralph's wife Margaret and Bey became good friends as the years went by; they even belonged to the same book club. How they would have fared sharing a kitchen will always remain a mystery, but that the families considered such a thing shows how different life was in those days.

Back then doctors made house calls—sometimes extraordinary ones. When I was only six and hospitalized with severe ear-infections, our family doctor was away on holiday in New York. Notified that the attending local physicians planned to perform a double mastoidectomy, he told them "No. I'm on the next train home. Wait." He took the night train and was back in Burlington the next morning examining me. His decision was *against* the surgery and he treated me medically until I was able to be released from the hospital, then continued house calls until I was completely restored. I'm not sure he was ever able to complete his vacation. Those were the days, as I said.

While in the hospital I received blood transfusions several times. It was very personal—the donor lying on one gurney, and just across the room on a parallel gurney the recipient. Blood flowed through overhead tubes—clear, small and transparent—from one to the other. I was aware that I was receiving this gift of blood, and in my case both donors were friends of the family. *Now,* I reckoned in my child's mind, they were more than friends; they were "blood-kin." No one *told* me that they were; I just figured it out for myself. One of the donors was a good Baptist lady who talked incessantly in a loud voice. The other was our across-the-street neighbor who came home every afternoon and bounded up the stairs two at a time. So . . . my childhood blood-fantasy played itself out in appropriate behaviors for one related to the donors: I practiced leaping up *our* front stairs two at a time; I also practiced talking more—and louder.

There was great excitement in the neighborhood when our next-door neighbor Mrs. Garrett had a baby. I was beside myself until we could go over for a visit and I could see this newborn wonder for myself. That was just the beginning. Having been told that they had brought the baby home from the hospital, I wanted to go immediately and get one for our family too. That must have been where the little book *Growing Up* proved useful to my mother. I still have the slender volume on my bookshelf. It tells you all you need to know. From this time on, I began to pray fervently for a little brother. I grew so exasperated after several years had passed without an answer that I finally said in desperation to the Lord, "Please send me a little brother, but if you don't have one of those, just send me anything you've got!" (In 1936, brother Jim was born, and in 1940, sister Nancy. God is good!)

There were some things about our life on Tarpley Street that I never knew at the time. One concerned our back-yard vegetable garden. Here my mother grew turnip greens to barter in return for milk and eggs at the local grocery store. She did this so that I could have milk to drink. Years later I would find myself thinking about that a lot: just how hard times had been, just how much my parents loved me and worked to see that I received things necessary to my health and well-being.

There were moments of social awareness on Tarpley Street, too. There was the day Helen Lea came over from her house to display her new and very shiny tricycle. Undoubtedly something Santa Claus had left, she was now showing it off—with a touch of class, if you get my meaning. "Where is *your* new tricycle?" she inquired, glancing at the dusty slightly rusty one I was riding. Without missing a beat, I looked down at my trike and responded,

"Well . . . what's wrong with *this* one?" Please note that I was not so self-aware as to have remembered this absolutely stellar answer. It was *Bev* who overheard the conversation, and was proud of me for standing my ground against this incipient class oppression.

Kindergarten was awesome. Mine was two whole miles away, in the county seat of Graham. Ours was a small garden of kinder in the home of Mrs. Cook. My favorite part—really the *only* part I remember—was lying down on little Indian rugs, listening to classical music during our rest-time. This was my introduction to the world of classical music, and I drank it in like a thirsty sailor. "Where has all this beauty been hiding? How can it come out of this little machine and wash over me like a tide? Oh, thank you, Mother, for bringing me to this beautiful place." I can still recall Mrs. Cook's sweet face, and her teenage son Mac who later became a concert pianist.

And then there was school. Serious school: first grade, to be specific. My parents had scrimped and saved to have a beautiful portrait-photograph done of me while I still had my long golden curls and before I succumbed to the current bobbed-hair, practical look for school. The curls *were* beautiful—if I do say so myself—and I suffered for them. Every night my mother sat me down in a chair and brushed out my hair, from the roots if you please, to get all the tangles—since I had very thick wonderful and naturally wavy hair. So both she and I paid for those curls in spades. She had to put up with my screeches and groaning—because it *really hurt,* and I had to put up with torture for beauty's sake. But the curls? They had to go, now that I was entering first grade. They were impractical. Envision naughty boys waiting to get their hands on my head of gorgeous well-arranged curls. So, off to the barber-shop we went.

Are there no beauty-shops in town? No gentler, kinder places? Off we marched to the barber-shop, the no monkey-business shop. I was hoisted onto a very high off-the-ground seat, and swathed in an enormous white with pin-stripes apron which covered *everything.* Then the barber's work proceeded—the demon barber of Main Street. The good news is: he did not chop off my head, a la Stephen Sondheim. But, as he did his dastardly deed, the golden locks began to fall—at my right and at my left. *Plunk.* Onto the floor they fell—some of them eight inches long. I had spent my life cultivating these curls. And the curls were not all that was falling. Quietly, silently, big tears began to roll from my eyes down my cheeks and onto the barber's apron, where they were soaked up. My mother noticed. "What's the matter?" she asked. *If she doesn't know, there's no way I can tell her—not now.* "The hair is getting in my eyes," was my face-saving response.

Hillcrest School was two-and-a-half blocks away from Tarpley Street. Under ordinary circumstances my mother might have walked me to school on the first day—my daddy being at work in the lawyers' office. But the circumstances were not ordinary. In August our family had gone to the Carolina coast—"to the beach" as Carolinians are wont to say, to meet up with some of daddy's relatives for a holiday. Bey did not swim, so when she ventured out into the waves it was always with someone on either side of her, holding her hand for support and reassurance against the mighty Atlantic. One day a really big wave crashed down upon the trio of waders-in-the-water, and she was thrown awkwardly to the ocean floor. A vertebra in her back was fractured, and she was consigned to bed rest for six weeks to recover. Ma-ma, our beloved grandmother, came to help out on Tarpley Street for several weeks. And during this time school started. Who would walk me to school?

To the rescue: my daddy Leo did it. That day he truly became my knight in shining armor. Until this time I had entertained a rather weird philosophy about parents. When asked whom I loved most—my mother or my daddy—I was quick to respond, "My Mother." When *Bey* inquired why I said that, my response was, "*You're* my real mother; I'm only kin to Daddy by marriage." I'm still trying to figure that one out. But today, on the very first day of my very first year in school, my Daddy was there to walk me to school. I had a gingham dress on and an enormous red bow in my freshly bobbed hair. And he held my hand all the way to Hillcrest. I can still feel the warmth of his hand in mine, and the strong sense of his presence towering above me, guiding me every step of the way. If ever a child had a positive sendoff into an enlarging world, I did on that day. Had I been queen of a kingdom in royal procession, I could not have felt more exalted. It strengthens me even yet to think of it.

My first grade teacher was Birdie Cox, but of course that's not what we called her. She was Mrs. Cox, a middle-aged lady who attended the same Methodist Church where I went to Sunday School. First grade classrooms at Hillcrest were on the ground level, so you got the idea right away that there was nowhere to go but *up*—providing you did well and obeyed the teacher's instructions. I certainly tried to do that, but one day I had trouble with her larger-than-mine vocabulary. She said several times to me, "Please modulate your voice." *What does that mean?* Not being able to work it out for myself, I waited until supper time and asked my daddy. "She means you are talking too loudly," he told me. Then I got it. And from that day on, according to Daddy, he had to strain to hear me, as I took the teacher's direction so very much to heart.

My daddy treated me like a tender plant. He left the stern rod of discipline in the hands of my mother, though he stood solidly behind her in her applications of punishment. "Spare the rod and spoil the child" was her firm and scriptural conviction, and she was very consistent. That is why it puzzles me that when I had misbehaved and she went outdoors to pick a fresh and keen switch, I always hid under the same bed—knowing full-well she would find me and give me what I deserved. It was our little liturgy of punishment, and we went through it religiously. She scarcely needed to mop under *that* bed; as I kept the floor so clean with my repeated visits. My most egregious naughtiness happened at a birthday picnic-cum-swimming party at a nearby lake. It was *my* birthday, and one would have thought I could behave then if ever. But I found a dirty used paper cup and decided to have a drink of water from it. Bey decided that was *not* a good idea, and the battle lines were drawn. In the end I received a sound thrashing, and in a very public place. Testing my limits, I was. *Surely,* I thought, she would let me get away with something rather than cause a commotion on my *birthday.* Not so. Bey did not hesitate to cause the commotion. Ah . . . consistency, thou art a jewel.

> *O God, you have taught me since I was young,*
> *and to this day I tell of your wonderful works.*
> Psalm 71: 17

Five
Dance, Sing And Play

A voyage marked by music and movement was my journey through school years. Many melodies linger on. Mrs. Cook had planted good seed in kindergarten and the musical plant was beginning to grow as I studied, learned, performed.

There were dancing lessons: ballet and tap-dancing. Concerning the former, let me just say that being swathed in pastel chiffon makes a person *feel* graceful no matter what. I was also tall with long legs. Tap-dancing was fun. I was invited to perform at meetings of local men's civic clubs. By fifth-grade, music was being integrated into the rest of life—largely due to the teaching genius of Mrs. Nixon who drew history, geography and the arts together. We danced the Minuet 'round the Maypole, the girls dressed in 18th century dresses with hoop skirts and wearing powdered wigs. More and more I began to understand music as an expression of life, a gift to be shared.

My age of innocence came to an abrupt halt in seventh grade, the age of torturous "dances" given by groups of parents for their emerging adolescents who had already been subjected to ballroom dance instruction. Woe is me. Dancing was not the real problem. The boys were super-glued to the walls while the girls languished in hopes of being asked for at least *one* dance that night. Our good 'ole dads stepped up to the plate like knights in shining armor—trying as best they could to model for the boys what gracious and sociable behavior just *might look like,* since the boys seemed clueless. Woe is me. My idea of hell is to be sent back to a junior-high dance again.

Perhaps there was more hope for me as a singer. When our fourth-grade music teacher introduced us to the world of three-part singing I memorized all three parts of each song and couldn't wait to get home and teach them to my home choir: Aunt Jane, contralto, my mother Bey, and me on the middle part known as second soprano. Away we went, singing our way through elementary school. Bless Bey and Jane; they never *once* had more important things to do or complained about being my captive choristers. How blessed I was as a child. What positive encouragement I received. On Sundays I went to church with my Methodist daddy, whose work took him away from home during the week. My Baptist mother—theirs being a *mixed marriage*—felt it only fair that daddy and I have some priority times together on the weekends.

When junior-high grades at Hillcrest produced the operetta *Cinderella,* I was chosen to sing the title role. My Prince Charming was a tall handsome ninth-grader. Learning the melodic solo parts was easy enough, but the dramatization offered challenges, like getting comfortable with the prince's arm around me while we sang a mushy duet. Even holding hands seemed too much; but there I was. And there also was our dramatic coach Miss Morrow, English teacher and card-carrying old maid you could spot a mile off. How ironic that *she* was the one to whip me into shape about the propriety—indeed *the necessity*—of some semblance of amorous behavior. After all, this operetta was a love story. Without love or some reasonable facsimile there was no credible story. Given just a few more years, I would have *adored* having Prince Charming's arm around me on stage. Funny thing is: in college years we even dated for a time.

My fondest memory of those awkward teen years was the Methodist Youth Fellowship, where junior and senior-high students mingled at key times. Sunday evening services were planned *by* the youth *for* the youth. The occasional weekend retreat would be attended by the full teenage spectrum plus our young adult sponsors who seemed to sense what we needed. What we needed was to see kids a few years older than we were acting civilized and sensitive. That meant we too might make it through this hormonally charged jungle called adolescence.

New singing opportunities opened up for me in high school. As a junior I had another chance for a singing role, this time in Gilbert and Sullivan's *Patience,* subtitled *Bunthorne's Bride.* Now the competition was much stiffer, and I failed to win the day as Bunthorne's bride. Maybe it's just as well, since I was so tall and Bunthorne was a shrimpy little guy at least four inches shorter than I. The gal chosen to play Patience was dainty and had a beautiful soprano voice; it was a suitable match. I was given the part of Lady Angela, one of the ladies in the court. None of this would have happened were it not for a musical mover-and-shaker named Eva Wiseman, director of the music program for the Burlington City Schools. Enormously gifted as a choral director and coach, equally gifted as a charming public presence, she was behind the scenes a stern disciplinarian of those in her care, her students. She knew how to get results and got them. Fifty years later her influence can still be felt, as she laid a foundation upon which music teachers who followed her were able to build.

Miss Wiseman had encouraged and challenged me as a chorister—so much so that my musical advocate *Bev* arranged for me to have private voice lessons in town. Mrs. Huff was in her sixties at the time, with a well-trained, rich voice. With her I learned Italian art songs and some Schubert *lieder,* and loved every minute of it. Some Sundays she lured me away from my Methodist church to sing in her choir at Holy Comforter Episcopal. It was here that I fell in love with Anglican liturgy. It was not radically different from my experience in a Methodist Episcopal church, but there was just something about it that came together for me. During the communion of the people I sensed this reverence, this awe which had eluded me before now. The nation was embroiled in World War II, and several families had servicemen overseas. As communion concluded each Sunday we sang a prayer-hymn for peace—the same one on each and every Sunday. There was a holy hush in the worship space as we knelt together, choir and congregation, and sang:

> *O God of love, O King of peace,*
> *Make wars throughout the world to cease,*
> *The wrath of sinful man restrain,*
> *Give peace, O God, give peace again.*
> (Words by Henry Baker, 1861)

Suddenly I knew how it felt to be part of a praying people. Already I had been inspired by a woman in the Methodist choir whose face simply radiated joy as she sang. Sunday after Sunday I would seek out her face to see what praise *looked like*. Now I was sensing a corporate dynamic, an anointing that seemed to rest on the entire congregation gathered. We were praying—faithfully, fervently—for peace in God's world. My concept of worship was growing.

Playing the piano had also been a big part of my life starting at age eight. That was when *Bey* enrolled me for piano lessons with Fletcher Moore, a professor of music at Elon College—now University—who also taught a number of private students in the downtown mezzanine ballroom of the Alamance Hotel. I felt quite *uptown* when I walked ten minutes from our new home to the hotel, mounting the stone staircase to the mezzanine for my lesson. My first piano book had pictures as well as large-noted music on each page. The most memorable piece I learned early-on was called "Moonlight," with the picture of a sylvan stream winding through woods under a silvery moon. Mr. Moore showed me the composer's name and asked me if I could pronounce it. Drawing upon all my third-grade phonics skills, I studied the long word for a moment, then sounded it out confidently: "Beeth"—long pause—"Oven." I sat back on the bench, feeling pretty satisfied with myself until he told me it sounded like this: "Bay—Toe—Ven." He said it with a kindly smile on his face, and never *ever*, in the years I studied with him, made me feel stupid.

When I learned to play "Moonlight"—the first sixteen bars of the Andante from Beethoven's Seventh Symphony—I thought I had died and gone to heaven. Suddenly the world of harmony opened up to me in all its glorious splendor. I felt again what I had felt on the Indian kindergarten rug: *where has all this beauty been hiding?* I was ravished by the sounds.

Several years later Fletcher Moore arranged for four of his piano students to give a joint recital in Whitley Auditorium at Elon College. This meant performing on a stage, not in somebody's friendly living-room, but a high and lifted-up place which you had to enter from backstage—a place familiar to *real* performing artists. It also meant performing more than one piece. In my case it meant several groups of pieces, with intervening spots covered by the other girls. This may have been my first serious experience of stage-fright. Nothing drastic happened; I was able to carry on even when my memory suddenly went blank and I resorted to repeating some familiar bars, hoping no one would notice until *yes—there it is*! My memory clocked back in and away we went for the finish line. Perhaps this initial plunge into improvisation prepared me for my love of playing music by ear, which began about this time.

As the years went by there was much dancing and singing and playing. I also discovered a certain dramatic gift which had lain dormant until now. It came to light in Miss Wiseman's girls' chorus. We sat on risers, some distance from the director. One day when I had a terrible sore throat, I faked it out and *pretended* to be singing. I knew full-well what pleased Miss Wiseman was to see students' tonsils as they sang. She frequently had us insert three fingers vertically into our mouths to get us accustomed to the idea. So I mouthed all the words of all the songs attentively and applied the three-finger rule right the way through class. Towards the end of the period Miss Wiseman stopped the chorus and said, "Now I observe that many of you are putting very little energy into this business of singing. *If all of you were working at it like Betty Jane back there, I would be hearing a different sound.*" Indeed she would have; she would have heard the sounds of silence, as I had mimed the entire thing. Having discovered this dramatic skill, I tried out for the senior play, which turned out to be lots of fun.

Now that I was a self-assured senior, dancing with boys was fun too. One boyfriend was a fantastic jitter-bugger. Boy, could he dance. Wearing the bell-bottom trousers of the day, he twirled me about the floor and made me feel like a pro, which I certainly wasn't. In preparation for the junior-senior prom my daddy provided my slow-dance preparation by sweeping me around our living-room floor in a graceful waltz. I in turn instructed my escort in the very same living-room before we went to the prom. His name was Joe and he was a fine student, but socially shy and without experience on the dance floor. We made it through the evening nonetheless—all of which reminds me that my boy-friends were out of the ordinary. For a start, I didn't have many, though I was a good pal with lots of boys at school. But I seemed drawn to boys who were either *outsiders* or from a different side of the tracks. I wonder why.

Let them praise his Name in the dance;
  let them sing praise to him with timbrel and harp.
For the Lord takes pleasure in his people,
  and adorns the poor with victory.
Psalm 149: 4-5

Six
A Tarheel Bred

"I'm a Tar-heel born,
and a Tar-heel bred,
and when I die I'm a Tar-heel dead!"

So sang we in *Hark! The Sound of Tar-heel Voices,* the UNC anthem. There was something infectious in the soil of North Carolina, something affecting the very soul of North Carolinians—inspiring great allegiance, great enthusiasm, great devotion. Maybe that is why I chose a college which was part of the Carolina university complex. My daddy favored a smaller college; there were several on his "to-be-considered" list, but the only in-state school on *my* favored list was Woman's College of the University of North Carolina, popularly known as "W.C." When questioned about why I wanted to go to such a big school, I said,

"Well, Daddy, it's a big world and I may as well begin to live in it."

That seemed to pacify him, and it was a brilliant answer for someone who had dedicated his life to public service. He had respect for that answer. My mother Bey deserves credit for reminding me years later that I had said this—I would never have remembered. It certainly got me off the hook with my dear ole' dad. He still had a problem with my majoring in music, sticking to his assertion that it was "one of the least lucrative professions in the world." I am convinced it was Bey's behind the scenes lobbying for my heart's desire that won the day.

Still, unbeknownst to me, during my first semester they wrote a letter to Dean Altvater at the School of Music, expressing their uncertainty—my dad's, really—about my having sufficient musical ability to major in music. The dean wisely waited until the first semester was nearly over, then, armed with test results in my music courses—all "A's"—he wrote them a very favorable and encouraging letter, and told them he thought I was eminently qualified to pursue a career in music.

That is exactly what I did. A Bachelor of Science in Music was a very focused degree program for those intending to be musicians. I yearned for more enrichment through the liberal arts, so I spent several summers attending sessions in Greensboro or at UNC, Chapel Hill, to take those sorts of courses: history, political science, German, philosophy, etc. This rounded me out academically, but when I was nominated as "Miss Watermelon" in a summer beauty contest in Chapel Hill, it was a bit too much rounding out for my taste. Still, the infusion of more liberal arts mitigated those endless hours holed up in practice rooms perfecting—*improving, if you will*—my instrumental techniques on the piano. Without those add-on courses I would have left college feeling intellectually impoverished.

By the sophomore year, having survived the rigors of freshman rules—enforced study in your dorm room from 7:30 until 10:30 every weeknight, lights out at eleven—things began to loosen up. By then presumably we had all learned good study habits and were totally dedicated to the academic tasks at hand. Maybe so, maybe not, but rules were more relaxed. There was more to life than studying and practicing the piano. There were quarterly dances given by the college societies. Though there were no sororities at W.C. on philosophical grounds, every young woman was a *de facto* member of one of four societies, whose purpose was primarily to sponsor social events. Including all students in something of a social nature went along with my egalitarian background. However, the societies were not fertile ground for forming friendships, as sororities can be: they were too big for that. They did bring young men onto the campus on some weekends, which was a good thing. One of the social alternatives for W.C.'s young women was to go see a boyfriend at one of the universities in Chapel Hill or Durham, where they *did* have fraternities and sororities. A weekend visit there meant arranging a place to stay. It also insured testosterone-driven activities much higher-keyed than the typical ones in Greensboro.

Dorm life was really where you got to know people more intimately. Having survived my freshman year with an assigned room-mate, a greater challenge now faced me. My chosen sophomore roommate was a precious girl from eastern Carolina, also a music major, who turned up pregnant before the end of the first semester. I had not come to college prepared for this. I had not a clue what to do—if anything. We simply co-existed, and although I feel sure she would have opened up to share some feelings had I encouraged it, the words, the questions, the invitation to share simply would not come out of my mouth. So steeped in "right" and ladylike behaviors, I was powerless in the face of a clear violation of those. I feel sure I was not unkind to Sonia by refusal to speak or avoiding her in the hallways. But I *did not reach out to her* in what was bound to be an embarrassing—at the very least—situation. I was totally impotent when it came to empathy. This has troubled me in later years as I see, through the 20/20 vision that hindsight often affords, the missed opportunity to show compassion in that situation. I was young and completely unprepared for this, or so I tell myself. May I never offend the heart of God again by such callous behavior. For her part, Sonia dropped out of school at the end of the sophomore year.

During junior and senior years at W.C. my friendships broadened to include several liberal arts majors—gals who were not stuck like glue to practice rooms in the Music Building. This was refreshing. Also, Jean, a classmate and piano major, loved playing by ear, as I did. We played exhilarating two-piano arrangements of semi-classic and popular tunes, and were even invited to perform on a local radio show in Jean's hometown, Winston-Salem. What fun! Our mutual pleasure in playing together paid off. When the time came to perform a movement from a piano concerto on our graduating recitals, we had no trouble choosing each other to play the second piano, orchestral reduction part. Making music *with* other people has always been one of my greatest joys. Whether accompanying the college choir, or playing in a chamber music ensemble, or playing duo-piano stuff with Jean, the *together* experience was for me so much more rewarding than solo piano work.

Singing together was the same: *more* fun to be a part of a group or choir than to warble away on your own. So Sundays would frequently find me riding to Burlington with a small group of college students of Walter Vassar, my voice teacher and coincidentally the new choir director at the now-familiar Holy Comforter Church twenty miles down the road. Though still a Methodist, my musical contacts seemed to be drawing me more and more in the direction of the Episcopal church. What would be next?

> *Know this: The Lord himself is God;*
> *he himself has made us, and we are his;*
> *we are his people and the sheep of his pasture.*
> *Enter his gates with thanksgiving;*
> *go into his courts with praise;*
> *give thanks to him and call upon his Name.*
> *Psalm 100: 2-3*

SEVEN
THE HANDSOME CANADIAN

Enter Graham Pulkingham. He is something of a lone ranger himself, having wandered all the way to Texas from his fatherland in Ontario. His appearance is dazzling—finely chiseled features, penetrating blue eyes and gorgeous platinum blonde hair to top it off. I do not remember having heart palpitations; there were other people in the office at the time and work to be done. My second full year as an Instructor at U.T. was beginning. Fortunately, the blonde Greek god was not assigned to one of my classes, or I might have been sorely distracted. By the luck of the draw he was placed in Shirley's class. Of course, I did have men in my classes; I even had a retired Army colonel, back from World War II and pursuing courses of interest. But Graham was different. From the start he was different.

Little by little, I found out interesting details about his background: how he had grown up as the only son in a family with four sisters, an agnostic father from Scots Presbyterian roots, and an adoring mother who had lost twin sons as infants before he was born. His mother was a devout Roman Catholic, so in her heart of hearts Graham was *already* a priest, since every good Irish Catholic family needed to produce one. A non-athletic, bookish sort of boy—the sort who read the dictionary or encyclopedias for fun—he attended a Jesuit school where nuns could mete out harsh punishment for minor offenses. He served as an altar boy from an early age, put on lots of weight as a pre-adolescent, then slimmed down in his teens into this gorgeous creature I was now beholding.

What brought him all the way to Texas, and how did he end up in the music theory office? He was twenty-four years old, no ordinary freshman, though signed up for freshman courses. It turns out his music pursuit was a post-graduate lark. He had grown up in Hamilton, Ontario and graduated from the University of Western Ontario with a pre-med course behind him. He was then given three choices by his father, who had in mind a sum for investing in Graham's future. One: he could join the family British-owned pottery business. Two: he could pursue training for the medical profession. Three: he could take the money coming to him and get lost, i.e., do whatever pleased him. Graham, like the prodigal son and many others who have left home on a quest for *something else,* chose the last.

His first stop was Nashville, Tennessee, where through some good fortune he was adopted into the summer art-colony/household of the famous American composer Roy Harris. *Eureka.* It was an exciting and thoroughly stimulating experience, but *way* over Graham's head in some ways. It was not that he couldn't comprehend the music *in his head.* He had spent years poring over recordings and scores of Beethoven symphonies and sonatas, his enthrallment dimmed only slightly by his mother's housecleaning frenzy while he was away at college when she had given away his entire LP collection of Schnabel playing Beethoven. No, he had a masterful comprehension of music *in his head;* he just lacked any practical way to express or work with it, like playing an instrument, singing, writing down the music. Enter the rudimentary theory courses offered by my friend Shirley. Graham had decided to go to Austin after meeting Keith Bardin, the Episcopal chaplain to U.T. students there. Keith convinced him that not only could he find the music courses he needed in Austin; he could pursue his theological bent there as well.

Over the next few months Graham and I became friends. Some of our earliest "dates"—if you could call them that—consisted of my hanging out at Canterbury House, the off-campus center for Episcopal student activities, and listening to Graham and Keith have theological word-battles. At a certain level it fascinated me; I had never been around people so keenly interested in these things and so familiar with theological lingo. But down deep it offended the sweetness-and-light Methodist in me. I was totally unprepared for these high-level arguments about God, nor was I sure the Lord was relishing them either. I seldom entered the fray, though occasionally asked a question. It was like watching a tennis game as the volleys went back and forth.

There were, thankfully, more pleasant interludes at Canterbury House, where Graham and several other students were rooming at the time. One of them was a guy named Hale Newcomer, which was good for chuckles. By hindsight, it seems to me that the newcomer who was really being hailed was Graham himself; but that is a personal interpretation colored by subsequent years and events. Canterbury House was a spacious, gracious old home with plenty of sitting and visiting areas, plus a grand old—old grand—piano where Graham tried out harmonic licks he had learned from the Harrises. These were times I enjoyed. I also enjoyed talking to him about his own background. His maternal grandparents were as Irish-Catholic as it gets with a name like *Sweeney.* Graham could recall his grandfather's stern disposition and his grandmother's having a parlor full of *mustn't touchables,* putting a damper on his childhood curiosity. His paternal grandmother, on the other hand, was Mary Graham McBride, about as Scottish as it gets. She lived with his family in later years and was absolutely devoted to Graham. She considered herself his personal laundress, sneaking into his room at night to retrieve clothes that needed washing, washing them, ironing them and having them outside his door the next morning. When she became ill and was taken to the local Catholic hospital, she referred to the nurses-cum-nuns as "black witches," revealing her own prejudices.

Clearly, religious differences had played an important part in Graham's past. He would describe the memorable knuckle-rapping nuns who taught him, and recall his school-mates, many of whom came from Hamilton's working class and not from the privileged neighborhood where his family lived. He had felt drawn to these peers, but cultivating friendships with them was not on his mother's list of approved activities. So he had turned to books and music for his enrichment, having no particular athletic inclinations. He literally *read* encyclopedias cover to cover and acquired an impressive library of musical recordings. Now, years later, he was introducing me to the world and thinking of Thomas Aquinas. All I remembered about *him* from college days was that his theology was based on Aristotelian thought. Now I was talking to someone who seemed to know him up close and personal, being thoroughly in touch with how his mind worked. Graham had attended a Jesuit high school before he left for university and subsequently broke away from the church entirely. The latter was a development abhorrent to his mother, who had raised him to be a priest and that was that.

Singing turned out to be a source of great pleasure for us both. During my first year in Austin I had sung in the choir at historic St. David's, Austin's downtown Episcopal church, where traditionally the organist/choirmaster also taught at U.T. By 1950 a new Episcopal mission started, and Shirley drafted both Graham and me into her start-up choir at St. George's. At Christmas we sang carols around the piano in Shirley's apartment, in the company of several others: Keith, my apartment mate Annabelle and her boyfriend. There were no chestnuts roasting on an open fire; thank goodness—this was central Texas and you were lucky to find a day of sweater weather. But we popped corn and strung it, strung cranberries and decorated a small table-tree while Keith mixed up the eggnog. Those were days of simple and rather basic pleasures.

Occasionally—this is to say, *very* occasionally—we actually drove in a car, though neither of us owned one, to an exciting evening event. One night we double-dated and drove to San Antonio to an opera performance. First we had dinner at a Chinese restaurant where I ordered sweet-and-sour pork, never having tasted it before. The lights went out just as dinner was served. How aromatic and romantic. An unfamiliar dish in an unfamiliar setting in an unfamiliar city can give you indigestion; but I remembered the dinner more than any other part of the evening—except for the ride home in the back seat. I can't recall what the opera was, or even the other couple. This was what Shirley later referred to as our *Tristan und Isolde* stage—Graham's and mine. We had definitely fallen in love, and were oblivious to much else around us. That became clear in the back seat, where on the way back to Austin we began to talk seriously about the future.

Before the spring was out we were engaged. But not before we had had some earnest discussions; you might call them disclosures. Mine were fairly ordinary: I had dated a lawyer back in Carolina and he had asked me not to make any other commitments until I came back home in the summer; but I don't recall that I had promised. A year before, a fairly steady dating relationship with a medical student had broken off because he was looking for a *wife*, not a woman building a reputation professionally. That was the end of that. And now?

Graham had more complex disclosures to share. He told me about some of the girls he had dated back in Hamilton where he grew up, and one older woman who—if I understood him aright—had taught him how to make love. But he also told me about a close pal in high-school, a guy for whom he had a very deep and continuing affection, and he asked me what I knew or thought about homosexuality. I said, "All I have heard is that it is the way some people are born, and you can't do much to change it." That was true. My information had been scanty; my experience nil. Graham's teen-age friend was now grown and married, with a family. Anyway, that was then and this was now. When all was said and done, it was clear to us that no matter what, in spite of potential hurdles or obstacles in our way, in spite of things beyond our ken, we were somehow meant to be together. We wanted to be together, we wanted to build a life together, we wanted to get married—in the sight of God and witnesses. That was our truth.

Now the hard work began—the work of getting our families' blessing and approval. My task was easier than Graham's. I had been writing home to my mother Bey about my exciting new friend, and she, being no stranger to youth and love, spotted a true romance when she heard about one. The only stipulation I recall my family laying down was that, if we were serious, the young man involved should come to North Carolina to meet my parents *first*—before I went to Ontario to meet his. This was social protocol in the south, but the plan didn't fly so well north of the border, as it turns out.

In a letter written June 6, after we had both gone home for the summer, hopefully to prepare for marriage before we returned to Austin, Graham said, "I'm so glad your family wants me in N.C. first—on many accounts. I'm afraid it's not just financial difficulties that's bothering Mom, but she's being plain on'ry." In the end, his mother did relent and he did come, but clearly she was not viewing me as a welcome addition to her only son's future. Indeed, I was an absolute threat to his becoming a Roman priest—and what other kind was there? The lines were drawn.

The keen vision of hindsight makes all of this intensely obvious now, but then it was vague, less articulated than *felt*. The feelings were acute for me when it was my turn to visit Graham's family in Hamilton. Though there was civility, there was minimal chatty conversation or anything that could have helped me relax. Things felt stiff, even icy at times. I chalked it up to a regional difference; this was, after all, not the sunny south. People didn't just sit around and chat informally and easily. I really had not and did not put it together: the truth of the matter was, they were extremely disapproving of this match, but too genteel to out and out *say so*. So I simply thought, "This is the way things are in Canada—it's not warm and fuzzy, and that's just the way it is." As it turned out, I had one silent advocate in the group: Graham's father. Though not able to come right out and say so, he was anything but sympathetic to the strict Catholic strait-jacket his wife seemed to have cut out for Graham.

So much so that he made his *own* trip to Carolina later in the summer—to see me again and meet my family for himself. He really wanted Graham to be free to make his own choices, and obviously didn't think I was an altogether bad apple. He saw me at the worst possible time cosmetically: when I had just had four impacted wisdom teeth removed, and was still in hospital recovering and scarcely able to move my jaw. I will always be grateful to Graham's dad Bill Pulkingham for making that trip. He was standing up to his wife, and for his son. That was a good thing.

Not all of my Canadian visit had been heavy and arduous. There were lighter moments, like joining Graham's parents and their distinguished visitor Sir Ernest Johnson for dinner at a Hamilton restaurant. Sir Ernest was in Canada on business for his firm Johnson & Brothers, of which Sovereign Pottery was a Canadian subsidiary, managed by Graham's dad. As we ordered our appetizers the international flavor of the gathering became obvious. Heads buried in menus, we ordered: first Sir Ernest ordered *to-mah to* juice, then Graham's mom ordered *to-maeh-to* juice, and I ordered *to-may-to* juice. Then we all looked up and chuckled. We were served identical juices.

Down in the sunny south preparations were in high gear in anticipation of a September first wedding. I feel sure there are simpler ways to pull off a wedding, but my experience has been that none of them turns out to be all that simple, no matter how small and unassuming you wish the wedding to be. Elopement may be the only way to insure simplicity. In the south there were certain expectations socially, and ours was definitely a *southern* wedding. There was a wedding director, a close friend of the family who had gentility oozing from every pore. She also knew what she was doing. There were pre-nuptial parties hosted by friends and climaxed by a cake-cutting on the night *before* the wedding. There were attendants: four bridesmaids, a junior bridesmaid, and groomsmen.

The junior bridesmaid was my ten-and-a half-year-old sister Nancy, who spent a good part of the summer in hiding—not because she didn't want to be in the wedding. On the contrary, she was excited about it, and fascinated by the accumulation of gifts that kept being delivered to my parents' home and displayed in the library. Here large sheeted tables were covered with beautiful pieces of silver, crystal, china, so that guests who happened to "drop by" could be invited in to see them; this was a *very* southern custom. Unbeknownst to anybody, Nancy would crawl under one of the tables before guests arrived, taking with her supplies like Nancy Drew books, cards and snacks. She would literally camp out for hours, just to eavesdrop on the *ooh*-ings and *ah*-ings going on overhead. This way she learned a lot about weddings without having to ask many questions. A smart kid.

Graham and I had fallen in love not only with each other, but also with the Episcopal Church, as it turns out. We had come to it from different directions: he from a Roman Catholic background and I from Methodism. After several years of exposure to the liturgical rhythm of the Episcopal Church, I felt I had simply walked into a larger room. Nothing that I found there violated or opposed what I had learned as a Methodist; it just seemed to take me deeper into the meaning of it all. As for Graham, I think he had found a church with basic orthodox beliefs but without the iron-clad rules that typified the Roman church. The difference was epitomized by our friend Roland Walls years later, when he found himself swimming the Tiber in the *opposite* direction, converting to Rome from the Anglican camp. He said, "It's like walking from an airy veranda with lightweight porch chairs, into a dark parlor with heavy overstuffed furniture. I keep bumping my shins."

Well, Graham didn't like bumping his shins; here in Anglicanism there was more freedom to explore, and he was an explorer. So, together we explored what it would mean to become Episcopalians in the fullest sense. Clearly, it seemed to be what God was doing in our lives. We were already attending services in an Episcopal church, more and more of our friends were pointing us in this direction, and—most importantly—

Graham's theological quest had come to the attention of Bishop John Hines who was functioning as recruiter-*extraordinaire* for a new seminary-in-the-making in Austin. With some trepidation but with my encouragement, Graham responded affirmatively to the bishop's invitation to become part of the first class at the Episcopal Seminary of the Southwest.

So it was that we were married at the Episcopal Church of the Holy Comforter in Burlington on September 1, 1951. This was my hometown, this was the church I had attended intermittently during high-school and college years. This was a good place for us to be married. Through memory's fifty-year mist, several things stand out: the darkened interior of the church—it was an evening wedding, the parish choir leading us in singing *Now Thank We All Our God . . . who from our mother's arms hath blessed us on our way with countless gifts of love, and still is ours today.* These words still sing themselves in my head. I remember the wedding processional, *March of the Priests*, from *Alceste*, chosen because it was *not* Wagner's overused march from *Lohengrin* and we liked the noble simplicity of the music itself.

It intrigues me that Graham and I came together that night to the strains of a reformer's music. The Bohemian composer Christoph Gluck is remembered as the Great Reformer of opera, breaking away from the ornamental musical style of the day and returning to earlier principles where music was subservient to the drama. In many ways Graham himself was a reformer, and took a radical turn away from the prevailing trends of his day: for him music was always subservient to the liturgy, supportive of it. It was never "show-off" time. All those fragmented attempts of his to learn music paid off through the years in his growing sensitivity to what music could *do* in worship. But that all happened later.

For now, we were married and on our way to New Orleans for a three-day honeymoon on route back to Texas. First stop: a hotel twenty miles up the road in Greensboro, where we both collapsed into bed exhausted but for different reasons. Graham, for his part, had been dancing an emotional tightrope due to his mother Marion's highly charged presence at our wedding, though she had certainly put up a brave front for most of us to see. Little did I know—until much later—how close we had come to missing her presence entirely, due to the rigid demands of her bishop concerning participation in a Protestant service. The story goes that Graham's dad had given the bishop a choice: between having his wife attend, or dealing with a divorce in the family. I, for my part, had barely recovered from extensive dental surgery and ensuing infection six weeks earlier. The swelling in my jaw had never altogether disappeared, and I felt tired most of the time. Fast forward: the next morning when I awoke, my right cheek was all puffed out again, chipmunk-style.

"Oh, no," Graham exclaimed. "The man at the desk is sure to think I hit you." The man at the desk was the least of my worries; I just wanted to know *what are we going to do now?* The obvious answer to that question was: go back to Burlington, get in touch with the oral surgeon, get more antibiotics going, etc. This was Plan B, which is precisely what we did, staying with my parents until we had worked out a treatment plan and were able to be on our way again.

New Orleans ho! Of course, we were traveling in the best man's car—we did not own one—and I feel sure our delay in Carolina constituted his inconvenience back in Texas. What a brave little band of Texans they were who had driven all the way from Texas for our wedding, and this long before the days of speedy inter-state travel. There were five of them, driving two cars so we could have one to drive back. They were: Keith Bardin, the best man, Bruce Jones, a groomsman, and friends Lillian Corner with daughter Rosemary, and Jo Ann Bennett— later to be wed to Keith. What a labor of love, to come all that way for us.

My chief memory of New Orleans this time around was going at long last to *Antoine's* for dinner. We drew the haughtiest waiter on staff; there's no doubt of it. I knew *some* French, and Graham knew more, but we did need help understanding a few items on the menu. Help was not forthcoming—only a disdainful glance coming down the nose of this waiter. We enjoyed our dinner in spite of him, and left an insulting tip as we departed. So much for a long-awaited visit to a world-famous restaurant. The medium is the message, *n'est pas?*

At night when we went to bed we began the serious business of *talking* about sex. We didn't have intercourse, but we did a lot of talking about it. Why? The most obvious and easy-to-talk-about reason was that we both realized the implications of intercourse: that I could get pregnant. *Laugh if you must.* Under our planning for the near-future, Graham was to enter first-year seminary and I was to support us on my Instructor's salary at U.T. So pregnancy was counter-intuitive at the moment. Contraception was not on the table for discussion because of Graham's Roman Catholic upbringing, and because I had respect for that and thought it made a lot of God-sense; and besides all that, I was pretty ignorant of any other thinking on the subject. So we began to explore the rhythm method, bought a thermometer so I could take my temperature and study my cycle. And . . . we waited. This was a honeymoon without a consummation of the marriage. The latter would come later.

But . . . we were officially married, and on our adventuresome way—both of us far, far from our families of origin. We were pilgrims on a journey, not remotely aware of what remarkable things lay ahead in God's plan for us.

> *Great things are they that you have done, O Lord my God!*
> *How great your wonders and your plans for us!*
> *There is none who can be compared with you. (Psalm 40: 5)*

Eight
Matrimony 101

An upstairs apartment on San Gabriel Street was our first home. Sparsely furnished, but at least we didn't have to haul around lots of *stuff*. There was a certain freedom in that which I could scarcely appreciate at the time. Now I do.

Down to the business of making a life together: There were meals to prepare, clothes to wash, transportation needs to address. And then there were the more intimate issues including sex, as well as a host of thoughts and feelings to share as time went by.

Clothes to wash? Ah, yes, there was Granny Corner. We'll start there.

Lillian and Dick Corner were an older couple, members of All Saints Episcopal Church, who lived near the university and seminary. Somehow—don't ask me how, I haven't a clue—Lillian took us on as her charge to keep. That is to say, she befriended us in no uncertain terms. Nothing with Lillian was uncertain. She was a quintessential Texas woman, tall, strong and angular, with a jaw line that could knock down a prize-fighter, and a personality of sandpaper. She also had a heart of gold. So she adopted the newly-wed seminarian couple and set out to find ways to serve our needs. She didn't have to look far to see the laundry piling up. Once a week she would come collect all our dirty clothes, take them home with her, bringing them back clean and dry and folded, with some wry comment like, "I'm sorry to hear your husband lost one foot already." Then she would hold up several one-of-a kind socks, to demonstrate her point.

Our apartment/home was not as close to the University neighborhood as either of us had lived before; still it was in the area, with regular bus service on Guadalupe, three blocks away. The bus was easy to catch, depositing me half a block from the Music building. Graham sometimes caught rides with seminary classmates—the ones fortunate enough to have a car—so he free-lanced his transportation needs. On the way home one or the other of us stopped off at the local corner grocery to pick up what we needed. This worked well for us.

One night Graham found it necessary to go back to the store unexpectedly. It happened like this: I decided to bake a cherry pie—my first ever. Perhaps to silence the inner voices murmuring, "*Can she bake a cherry pie, Billy Boy, Billy Boy?*" and to disprove the last line, "she's a young thing and cannot leave her mother." I had *already* left my mother, but she had not left me—without arming me with a host of recipes from her "never-fail" file. So here I was, baking my first-ever cherry pie. I have no idea what went wrong: Was it the oven that baked too hot? Did I misread the recipe? Let's just say that Billy Boy's pie was a total flop. And so was I, as far as I could tell. But Graham would not accept that for a moment. Like the trainer who helps the thrown rider re-mount the horse, Graham simply said, "Not to worry. I'll go to the store and buy some more cherries, and you can start over." That was the last thing I wanted to do, and the very best thing I could have done, because the next pie turned out fine. That was "Cooking School for Newlyweds—101."

Soon after we arrived from our extended—because of circumstances beyond our control—honeymoon trip, Graham received a letter from the seminary which seemed to trouble him. They wanted him to come have further talks with the psychologist, following the psychological testing he had undergone earlier. I never knew the specific result of all that, except that he did go for several months to see a psychotherapist to whom he had been assigned. She was someone he came to know as a friend—both her and her family, and he was very fond of them. But that is neither here nor there: the thing was, this therapy satisfied the seminary's requirements, and that was that. In the meantime, our marriage was consummated, and that seemed good. We were definitely "on track."

We each had work to do. Graham's work was at the seminary, which had no visible structure, classes meeting in Canterbury House, and some courses shared with students at Austin Presbyterian Seminary across the road. The Episcopal Seminary of the Southwest was definitely a shoestring operation, the brain-child of John Hines, Bishop of Texas and later Presiding Bishop of the Episcopal Church, USA. Credit is also due to Bishop Clinton S. Quin, his predecessor, for laying the groundwork. In what proved to be a prophetic vision in the fifties, Hines launched out to provide a place to train future priests for the Episcopal Church in the southwest—thus the name *The Episcopal Theological Seminary of the Southwest (ETSS)*. Priests were in short supply in the post-World War II era, and this institution, with all its ups and downs, appears to have fulfilled Hines' vision and supplied a real need. When I last saw John Hines at a seminary event a few years before his death, I hoped that he felt a sense of "well done, good and faithful servant."

On a day-to-day basis, life at the new seminary was grass-roots at its grassiest. The seven beginning students, *juniors* in seminary lingo, used to pour themselves into one vehicle and drive to the Night Hawk restaurant for mid-morning coffee. As I think about it now there is a big credibility gap imagining all of them in one vehicle. Maybe it was a van, or *two* vehicles. Anyway, these were pre-Starbucks days and the coffee was affordable. Two parish priests in the diocese drove into town each week to teach Old Testament and Church History, and the Dean who lived in Austin taught New Testament. Then there were professors of Greek and other courses at the Presbyterian Seminary, who took the fledgling group under their academic wings, filling out their curriculum.

My contact with the new seminary was minimal, as I was the working partner in the marriage, working on what was whimsically termed a "PHT"—putting hubby through—degree. Occasionally I went to some special evening gathering in Canterbury House. One of them engaged the topic of homosexuality. If I were now threatened with death in front of a firing squad, I could not possibly tell you what the content of the session was, only that I found myself terrified, flushed—with obvious elevated blood pressure—and mute. Out of my depth I was, with no vocabulary to describe what was going on inside of me. Once, as a college sophomore, I had been rendered speechless when I found out my unmarried roommate was pregnant. Nothing in my background had prepared me to deal with something so off the charts. Now, another *tabu* matter was confronting me. This issue was clearly not going away, as I had thought it would. Yet I was at a loss to know what to do with my feelings, so I simply "stuffed" them. They seemed to stay comfortably stuffed, except that once in a while they re-surfaced when Graham would catch a ride home from seminary with a particular classmate, and seem to spend *forever* sitting in the car outside talking—before coming in. Fear can be a paralyzing emotion, and I simply found no words to talk about this with Graham, no way to ask questions or express my feelings, or re-open the whole subject we had discussed and laid to rest before we were married. *No way at all.*

Meanwhile, down in the Music Building just blocks away, life was never dull—or at the very least not *nearly* as dull as what I had perceived the Master's course in Music Theory at Eastman might have been, had I stayed there. Dr. Irvine McHose had been a chemist before he was drawn into music, and his scientific methodology had students bent over Bach chorales for hours, counting tonic six four chords and such like. But here in Texas life was different, more casual, though definitely not slipshod. Dean Doty kept the thermostat turned into the sixties, and the story goes that he, being from Michigan, had remarked that southerners worked best when well-chilled. The actual quote was more like "You have to freeze southerners half to death in order to get a lick of work out of them." Well, I was chilly, and came to work armed with a heavy sweater which was necessary most of the time. The contrast when walking out into 100-degree heat was a shock to the entire system. Then I trundled home to an upstairs, *un-air-conditioned* apartment to *cook* over a hot stove, if you get the picture. We did buy a box fan, and if you had nothing better to do, you could sit and count the blade revolutions—that's how slow it was.

Back in the icebox where I worked there were lots of student recitals to attend. In addition there were freshman and sophomore theory classes to teach, slipping on the occasional banana peel in front of the whole class—it *did happen* once—grading papers and teaching piano to a few music education majors. The theory classes were fun for me, and there were several outstanding students who could have taught *me* a thing or two because of their God-given musical abilities. One was Kathleen Armstrong, now Thomerson, whom I came to know later in Houston. Another was Gerre Hancock, of St. Thomas' Church, New York fame. When I saw Gerre years later, he introduced me to a friend saying, "I want you to meet the woman who steered me through the vicissitudes of freshman theory." Great vicissitudes indeed; it was a snap for him.

Graham and I both loved singing, and singing proved to be the activity that drew together the two pieces of our lives: music and the church. We sang in the University Madrigal Singers for a time, and especially enjoyed being part of the York Cycle of mystery plays presented as chancel dramas at All Saints during Advent. Graham was perfectly cast as the Angel Gabriel in one of the plays. His platinum blonde hair, illuminated by special lighting and set off by his long white robe, made a dazzling appearance as he stood in the pulpit to deliver the startling message to Mary: "*Greetings, you who are highly favored! The Lord is with you . . . Do not be afraid; you have found favor with God. You will be with child and give birth to a son, and you are to give him the name Jesus. He will be great and will be called the Son of the Most High.*" The synergy between theology and music was deep and meaningful to us both; we were enriched, nourished by it.

This is my Story This is my Song

All Saints became our church home. Just weeks after we were married, a visiting bishop confirmed me and received Graham, who had already been confirmed as a Roman Catholic in his youth. Our rector, Scott Field Bailey, was a gentle and compassionate man, the perfect pastor for us. He and his parish championed the seminary's efforts to get up and running, and made parish facilities available for use whenever possible. How very fitting it is that the elegant mansion-home of the Villavaso family, who donated their estate as the building site for ETSS, is now called the *Bailey Center.*

Before long I was asked to become choir director at All Saints. The very proficient organist Virginia Decherd wanted to get rid of the choir aspect of her job—understandably, as she spent her days directing choral groups at Austin High School, and enough was enough. Also, involving with a scruffy band of volunteers in a church was a wholly different thing than riding herd over a class of kids who *had* to be there, and with Virginia as director, *had* to behave. I can still see those steely blue eyes which could penetrate like a laser beam: "If your mother didn't teach you any manners, *pretend* that she did—if you want to stay in this class."—was one of her tactics in behavioral modification for teen-agers. She could send chills down your spine and theirs. We had a good working relationship; of course now *I* was the one with the challenge of attracting new church choir members and keeping the old ones happy. Virginia just played the organ and gave me her Cheshire cat smile. One Sunday before the service I was so frustrated with poor choir attendance that I said to our rector Scott Field, "Tell these people if they want a choir, they better turn up and show me." To which the wise pastor replied without raising his voice, "I'll tell them *no such thing.*" That was an early lesson for me in pastoral care, and I've never forgotten it, or the beloved man who said it.

The summer was hard, as Graham was assigned field work with a Navajo mission priest in New Mexico. I was very much alone—still teaching in summer school, still without wheels and feeling at times emotionally abandoned. Early days at the seminary did not offer the possibility of student dorms which would have encouraged a sense of community. I don't recall any of the social gatherings in the Dean's or a student's home, which have been recounted by others. Maybe we didn't go because there was no easy way to get there, so Graham didn't bother telling me about them (?) I'll never know. But I do know how lonely I felt that summer. Our landlords, an elderly couple, later shared with Graham that they sometimes heard me crying in the night upstairs. Though that has faded from my conscious memory, it sounds right. Thank God for George and Mary Carlisle. Both of them were veterans of World War II, and George a classmate at the seminary; they took pity on me and invited me to spend several weeks in their home. What a gift of hospitality at a time when I felt so needy. The Lord is merciful.

The second, or *middler* year of seminary rolled around, and new challenges appeared on the horizon. Somewhere along the way Uncle Sam put in his bid for our attention. Up until this time Graham had been a dual-citizen of the U.S.A. and Canada, having been born in Ohio but having lived in Canada since infancy. Now, at age twenty-six, he was required by law to declare his citizenship choice. He chose American citizenship for fairly obvious reasons, since he had come to live and work in this country and had married an American wife. Before long the draft board was in touch to inquire about his draft card, a kind of "When do you plan to suit up and show up?" inquiry. This was the beginning of several months of conversations with them, with me, and considerable soul-searching about what to do. Most of his classmates were older men and veterans of the armed services. In the end, Graham decided the only thing that made sense for him was to go into service and fulfill the military obligation of being a citizen of the U.S.A. during wartime—the Korean War.

So it was *Anchors Away* for us, as Graham chose to serve in the Navy. It was springtime of 1953 before all this got sorted out and we did the necessary planning. By then there was another development which affected the future: I was pregnant. We were both delighted, if somewhat awed, by this. Graham came down with a case of German measles and promptly isolated himself in our second bedroom so as not to expose me. There were anxious days until that threat passed. So here was the plan: after completing the spring semester in our respective schools I would go to North Carolina for the summer to await the early September arrival of our first baby. Graham would remain in Austin to complete his summer assignment in clinical pastoral care at Austin State Hospital. Then he would join me in Carolina until the first stage of naval officers' training at New London, Connecticut, commenced.

For me, the timing was good: I had completed four years as an Instructor at U.T. and, having chosen marriage rather than further graduate study, I was subject to the "up or out" rule which applied to faculty after that time had elapsed. I was happy to be "out" and onto building a family, so it was a happy closure at the University. And—as it turned out—it was a good and maturing move for Graham also. So: *anchors away.*

First things first, there was a baby on the way. I settled into life back in Carolina for the summer months, checked in with our wonderful family physician, then went to the Smokey mountains for a week's approved holiday with my parents. I can still hear the "clomp-clomp" of clogging in the recreation hall near our lodging. The sounds carried with great resonance over the hills and down to the mountain lake. It was a peaceful and restful time, leaving me completely unprepared for the shock that followed upon our return to Burlington. I went into labor prematurely. Most likely the result of struggling to park in a tight parking place downtown, I began to experience labor pains on July 18. Hospitalized, I was given all the appropriate treatment to slow things down, but to no avail. I delivered a beautiful baby boy on July 20, seven weeks earlier than planned. He was named William Graham III, and we called him Bill, after his paternal grandfather by the same name. I was devastated by not being able to hold him or see him initially, as he was in an incubator and under close surveillance. My sense of having failed him was enormous; my tears flowed for what seemed an eternity, though it was only for a day—a very long and lonely day. No husband, no baby. Then I was better. The doctor said the baby, though he weighed just four pounds, six-and-a-half ounces, was "a little Ajax." He was a strong and healthy baby. A visiting friend assured me that she had been a *preemie* and placed in a shoe-box when she was born; and just look at her now—she tipped the scales well over 200 pounds. So clearly, there was life after premature birth. I began to feel relieved.

Back home at my parental home-place on Davis Street, I healed and we waited for the great day when the baby would be released from the hospital. There was a running dispute between the family doctor and pediatrician as to what weight little Bill must reach before being released. They were still sorting that out, as far as we knew, when the phone rang one day and Dr. Harden said,

"I am calling to let you know your son has been released from the hospital. The baby may come home now."

I was dumbfounded, suddenly awe-struck by the very thing we had been waiting for. Bey was standing near the phone as I talked to the doctor; she could sense my consternation, as I searched for some reason to delay—at least long enough to get my mind wrapped around it all. Suddenly she noticed it was raining outside.

"It's raining," Bey whispered to me, helpfully. Ah, yes, that's it—a brilliant observation.

"Dr. Harden," I said, "It's *raining* outside."

There was a long, pregnant pause on the other end of the line. Then he said, in his characteristic gentle manner, "Well, I can lend you an umbrella." Touché, as they say in France.

We collected the baby within an hour. And, praise be to God, we soon collected the baby's father upon his arrival from Texas. So all hands were on deck, which was a very good thing in the days that followed. I was so nervous because Bill was tiny and felt as if he could slip right through my arms. Graham was much calmer on task than I. Thank God he was here. Days flowed

This is my Story This is my Song

into weeks, and there was plenty for all of us to do. These were the days before washing machines were in great supply—at least, my parents didn't have one. Washing diapers by hand, triple-rinsing them, boiling them, hanging them on a line to dry, taking them down again and folding them: well, there's a piece of work right there. And that was just one of many things to do. Before long, Graham was off to report to the Navy, and we were not to see him again until Christmas. By then Bill was clearly going to survive—even by my up-tight standards. Things were getting easier. It would be spring before Bill and I were able to join Graham for the next phase of his naval training.

Recalling my days as a navy wife brings back a kaleidoscope of memories. There was Newport, Rhode Island, where Graham received special training to be a legal and personnel officer. Our shotgun apartment had a living room followed by a bedroom followed by a kitchen followed by a common hallway followed by a bathroom. *Nice.* Next-door lived a sailor and his Cockney wife and young son. We used to hear the culture-wars through paper-thin walls, the young mother trying to teach her son to say "please" while the sailor bawled, "Don't make the kid *beg.*"

There was a tiny kitchen, into which Graham brought three tremendous live lobsters, biding their time in a big bucket of water. He also brought home a couple of Navy buddies for supper, and put a large container of water to heat on the stove. We retired to the living-room for drinks, agreeing ahead of time that I would dunk the sea creatures in their last total immersion once the water had come to a boil. He would do the rest.

Well: Armed with a fairly large Martini, I retired to the kitchen in the fullness of time, hoping to fulfill my part of the bargain. The rest is a blur. As Graham loved to tell it, "After waiting a while I thought I'd best go check on Betty to see how things were going in the kitchen. There she was—perched atop the washing machine, peering down at the squirming and still very much alive lobsters in the buckets; she was obviously well-lubricated herself." That is the best eyewitness report I can give you, but I do remember thinking I had been assigned mission impossible. It would not be the last time in our marriage when I felt that way.

Before long we were on the Navy trail again, this time to Key West, Florida, where Graham was assigned as personnel /legal officer on a submarine tender. First we sandwiched in a visit to Lake of Bays, where the senior Pulkinghams had a cottage. It was my first and only glimpse of northern Ontario. Lovely. There were rampant tales about encountering bears on the way to the outhouse; these tales had become family lore over the years. Laundry facilities were fairly non-existent, so I washed baby Bill's diapers in the lake—for which I carry an enormous load of guilt for the eczema he later developed on one leg. Woe is me. Perfect parenthood is so hard, and mothers collect guilt so readily.

Southward to Carolina next, we visited my family and rooted around their basement for early-married furniture possibilities— you know, discarded items or damaged goods. Our greatest find was an old oak wash stand which had come from my grandparents' home. It had all the makings of a fine toy-chest for Bill, so I did what was popular at the time: I smothered it in black lacquer: *Voilà*. It was now *Early-married Oriental* and on its way to Florida. Graham preceded us by some weeks, and Bill and I followed on the train to Miami, then by a little prop plane to Key West. I'll never forget the flight, low enough in altitude that we could appreciate the coral reefs in their incredible display of color and shapes. Oh, and did I tell you? I was pregnant again.

> *Put your trust in the Lord, and do good;*
> > *dwell in the land and feed on its riches.*
> *Take delight in the Lord,*
> > *and he shall give you your heart's desire.*
> > > *Psalm 37: 3-4*

Nine
The Road Ahead

Following a snaking ribbon of highway south from Miami, you will see nothing save water on either side. If you keep going you will arrive in Key West a hundred and eighty miles later. Uncle Sam had sent Graham here as an officer on a submarine tender. That's a huge benign ship lacking the usual accoutrements of warships. Its warring counterparts are unseen beneath the surface: lethal submarines. All I know experientially is that when danger looms, as from an approaching hurricane, all the ships and officers depart. Waving "bye-bye" to wives and children, they take to the high seas. Wives and children can presumably fend for themselves. But . . . wait a minute: I thought in times of danger it was the women and children whose needs were looked after first. Not exactly, as it turns out. The U.S. Navy looks after its ships first of all; and in the case of an approaching hurricane, that means getting "out of Dodge"—out of port—onto the high seas to avoid the brunt of the storm when it makes landfall.

Nice work if you can get it; and we got it. Key West has a romantic Hemingway-esque ring about it. There are spots made famous by the author's visitations, spots which attract droves of tourists. I never saw the spots. I only saw Sigsbee Park, the naval housing development dredged up out of the bay. I saw the new shiny washing machine, our first appliance ever, listened to its sudsy hum and to Bill's great fourteen-month-old imitation. Standing by the washer, he chanted, "Koochee-

koochee-koochee-koo." And I felt the clothesline outside bend and sway under my hands as I hung freshly washed diapers three dozen at a time in the blazing sun, and heard the wind whipping through them, making them crackle. We now had *two* babies in diapers. As soon as diaper #36 was hung I could begin collecting diapers #1 forward; they dried within a couple of minutes. I heard the Havana radio announcer selling milk *con leche*—with top cream?—and wished I had studied Spanish instead of those languages from faraway places I would likely never see like France and Germany. Sometimes I wondered if Bill's first sentence would be in Spanish, with me needing an interpreter. Mary Graham was just eighteen months younger than her brother, and though I was only twenty-seven I frequently felt exhausted. If ever I managed to get the two of them down for a nap at the same time I made a run for my bed and *crashed*. One very special day was the day we purchased our first car. It was a used Plymouth sedan, and Bill loved to sit in the back seat and watch the street go by *underneath* through the rusted-out hole in the car's flooring.

The only time we ventured from Sigsbee was the night Graham and I attended Christmas midnight mass at St. Paul's Episcopal Church. There was a heavy cloud of incense in the church, and the thurifer had a game-arm which made it hazardous to sit next to the aisle. A colorful event, and I was so glad to be there, to sing hymns and carols, feeling once again the excitement of a festival service celebrating our Lord's nativity. With two babies at home and a husband at sea much of the time, getting to church was a rare and exciting event for me. Graham had organized a small choir of sailors on his ship who sang for services while they were at sea. All in all, as compared with our past experiences in Austin, we were somewhat disconnected church-wise, and we felt it. That would end soon enough.

With Graham's tour of duty in Key West finished, we headed for my parents' home in Carolina. Our main job now was to pick up the civilian pieces of our life and provide for a growing family. Meanwhile, there was seminary—on the back burner but needing to be re-addressed. Would Graham return to finish his third and final year there? He had long been intrigued with the graduate program in anthropology at the University of Chicago. Maybe he would turn out after all to be a perpetual student, fulfilling one of the concerns Dean Doty had expressed to me shortly after meeting Graham in his music student era; quoth the dean, "I hope he's not just a dreamer." Clearly, however, he was a complex guy with many capabilities and many possibilities to explore. So?

We both set to work to bring in some income. I did part-time secretarial work for a local lawyer who was a friend of my parents. After doing part-time substitute teaching in the local high-school, Graham, to my somewhat amazement, became a traveling salesman—one of those jobs that is open to curious or desperate people combing the pages of the classifieds. He sold Bibles briefly. Then he turned to sewing machines—a practical and needed household item in those days. The machines he sold were dirt-cheap. The deal was: after you sell this thing and get the money, you then show the hapless consumer that—incidentally—this bobbin has to be wound by hand, a very primitive and time-consuming endeavor. *But*—you hasten to assure the customer—you just happen to have with you a new and splendid machine that winds its *own bobbin*. Whereupon you show the beleaguered housewife, who is by now jostling a whining child needing to be fed, just how cool this machine really is. *And* . . . wonder of wonders, the money she has just paid you for the other machine will serve as an adequate down payment for the new one. Then you close the deal.

Graham could hardly sleep at night, pondering the ethical aspects of this job. Every bone in his body railed against this kind of manipulative and deceptive salesmanship. But there he was, needing work and income, so he did it for a time. Every day for him must have been a dose of castor oil. *Yuk*. I sometimes think it was the sewing-machine job that propelled him back into seminary. Because one night while staying in a cheap motel in eastern Carolina he was restless, probably dreaming about some poor family who had no bread for the children because the money had gone into payment for the sewing machine. He roused himself from sleep with something like unto a revelation: he would call Bishop Hines the very next day about returning to complete his year of studies leading to ordination. He did call, and the bishop assured him there was a place waiting for him. Eureka.

We went. By now the stage which life prepares for us was set. The stage was set for Graham the seeker's conversion. Being the highly intellectual sort that he was, it had taken a while to get to this place of decision, this place of surrender. Dr. Frank Young was the New Testament professor at the Seminary. Sitting in his class, listening to him teach from the Gospel of St. John, Graham found new life in Christ. Faith does indeed come by hearing the word of God. He heard it. It made all the difference. The somewhat withdrawn person, whose first student sermon at All Saints, Austin, had been torturous to witness, was transformed into a real preacher. That became obvious at our first mission church in Hitchcock, Texas, where Graham was assigned after ordination as a deacon. He was in love with the word of God, deeply moved by God's story, and able to communicate it and draw others into it.

He was now a licensed, fully equipped circuit-riding preacher. That is to say, he had three church assignments: to serve as vicar of the mission at St. John's, Hitchcock, the mission at St. Mark's, Alta Loma, and to be the Episcopal chaplain to staff and students at John Sealy Hospital, the University of Texas Medical Branch. None of the three were remotely alike. This made life interesting.

St. John's, Hitchcock was in a small town, amongst a stable population including several real "old-timers." We were fortunate to be able to stay with the Barker family—Owen and Enid—until the new rectory was completed about a month after our arrival. They were highly loved and respected older members, and their very presence lent an air of stability to life at St. John's. I was able to start a small choir, even though its membership was lopsided: six women, and just one male member. Still, it worked, and I loved writing out musical arrangements for our little group. It's just as well that I did, as we had no music budget whatsoever. The church building itself was a Quonset hut structure, strictly utilitarian. Four-year-old Bill told me one Sunday that he wanted his offering of coins to help get a steeple for the church. Obviously, he was recalling the beautiful Gothic structure at All Saints, Austin, and longing for some of those aesthetics to follow us to the Gulf coast.

St. Mark's, Alta Loma was made up entirely of young families who loved to get together and do *whatever* it took—cleaning, carpentry, cooking for church dinners, childcare, *you name it*. They just loved being together. The church was their social network. I frequently thought 'this must be what the early church was like'—this *koinonia*—this like-minded fellowship as God's gathered family. Years later I would look back thankfully for this momentary glimpse of the joy of Christian fellowship. How totally involving life in a small church can be—with all hands on deck. Graham conducted his first adult baptism service for a member of that congregation. Calvin was a really tall guy from a Baptist family who had married Elaine, a Roman Catholic, and the Episcopal church proved a good meeting place for the two of them. Calvin wanted to be immersed. I held my breath as minister and candidate waded into the water of a nearby Baptist Church baptistry. Calvin was about a foot taller than Graham, who had the responsibility of submerging him.

The third leg of this circuit-riding stool, the chaplaincy in Galveston, was mostly unknown to me, as it was down the road apiece and out of my range. However, I was soon to learn more, because after just one year on the circuit, Graham was asked to take on the chaplaincy full-time. This meant moving once more—from Hitchcock into Galveston. My reaction showed just how domesticated I had become: "But—what about the *draperies?*" This referred to the drapes my dear mother Bey had made when she visited, and which we had hung only a couple of months ago, having draped sheets over windows for the first six months. Graham's response was so cluelessly male: "The *draperies?* Why are you worried about the draperies?" *Well, if you don't know, there's no way I can tell you.*

    I would miss our Hitchcock home, which still smelled *new*. I would miss the brilliant red bottlebrush shrub outside and the choleas I had planted which grew like Topsy. One thing I would not especially miss was the sensation of living in a fishbowl, as we were next-door to the church and some of the church members thought nothing of coming to visit at awkward times. Our faithful collie Buddy would not even bark to warn me they were on the way, so friendly was he. None of the visiting neighbors had two young children to look after; but I had been so steeped in "south-e-ren" manners that I did my best to cover both fronts and not offend anyone. Besides all this, I was pregnant again as we prepared to move to Galveston. Would Bey come to our rescue and adapt the drapes? I surely hoped so.

    Of course she did. She was *always* there for us—rain or shine. This time, in Galveston, she set to work altering the draperies for entirely new windows. One day she needed a spool of thread. Graham and I were headed for Houston for an appointment and promised to pick up thread for her. At Gulfgate Mall on our way home, we visited Joske's. Surely this large department store would have thread. They did. They had *lots* of stuff. Our eyes fell on a sale of Thomasville furniture. That was a well-known North Carolina company, and I was drawn to their sturdy pecan pieces in Rural English style. We had no furniture to speak of—except for those pieces from Bey's basement, some Hollywood beds and a few chairs and oddments we had picked up. In a moment of real daring, we purchased a dining-room suite, a desk, coffee-table, two end-tables, plus a sofa—and, oh yes, the *thread*. This was our first credit experience—buying something we had no way to pay for today, but the monthly payments were set up, and we calculated we could handle it. We did—or should I say I did, as I was the monthly book-keeper and financier. The unusual ratio between our very low income and our very high debt just *may* have been the reason for next year's visit by the IRS. They were intrigued by it also. For my part, I can still remember the knots in my stomach at the end of every month, when the bills came due. How to juggle things *this* time around?

Back home from our unexpected splurge of spending, we handed Bey the thread, and told her *more* was on the way. She chuckled as she described listening in on the children's playtime that afternoon. Bill was playing "preacher" and Mary was sitting in the congregation with her baby doll. One of the recurring phrases in Bill's sermon was " . . . and nevermore, and nevermore, and nevermore."

Finally Mary piped up to inquire, "Bill, when can I say something?"

His prompt reply was, "Women don't speak in church."

Not to be put down so easily as that, Mary sighed, "Well, I get tired just holding this baby and saying *Amen*." Mary was a two-year old women's libber arriving just in time for a sea-change.

Looking back on our two years in Galveston fills me with nostalgia. There were memorable family excursions like crabbing in the bay area, or taking a picnic to the beach just up and over a hill from our house. Bill and Mary camped out in the front hallway when hurricanes blew in, the hallway being the only area protected from big glass windows. Always the sailor at heart, Graham would help me get the children bedded down, then go out to walk near the seawall and see the storm up close. He could have been a good reporter for the weather channel. Nathan, child number three, was one of those with B.O.I. on his birth certificate: 'born on the island' was the only way to be a *real* Galvestonian.

New professional opportunities opened up for both Graham and me. As he visited in the locked ward of the psychiatric wing of the hospital, he got to know the psychiatrists on staff, and became part of an experimental program labeled "multiple impact therapy." Though it is probably *old hat* now, at the time it was a new concept to involve a team of professionals in family therapy. The theory was that when a mental patient received treatment at the hospital and was simply sent home, most likely to the same dis-functional family environment that had contributed to the illness, the patient would rapidly relapse. The team approach offered help to the whole family so they could provide a therapeutic re-entry for the member who had been ill. This was exciting work for Graham; he was challenged and stimulated by it and by working alongside others in helping professions.

I had two memorable contacts with the psychiatric hospital: one very positive, and the other quite different. First there was James White, a nurse on the psychiatric wing. His name was White but he was black as the ace of spades, and one of the dearest friends to us. He was great with patients who had dementia, calling big dogs from underneath the beds of frightened patients, and shooing the dogs down the hall himself. He did off-duty nursing too, as when I came down with mumps at age thirty, and was really sick.

Then there was Mike, a teenage psychopath and out-patient at the hospital, who needed a place to stay temporarily while something was being worked out with his family. Graham invited him to come stay with us. I was about seven months pregnant with Nathan at the time, and I feel sure I must have agreed to it. But like many other times in life, you don't always know what you are getting into. Do you *ever*? Mike was not particularly disruptive to family life, as Graham kept a close eye on him, but he did have an annoying habit of roaming around the house at night and peering into the beds of those asleep. I found it most unsettling—read my lips: *terrifying*—to wake up and become aware of this *presence* looming over our bed. It's the only time I ever cried "Help" to my doctor, who prescribed a tranquilizer for me in the night hours. Mike did no physical harm to any of us, but it was scary nonetheless.

And then there was the handsome young married doctor. I found myself unaccountably drawn to him and sexually attracted—something I was not looking for. It was shocking to me that I *felt* this way about another man than my husband. Oh, help. There was no "acting out" on my part—and certainly not on his; he would have been totally unaware of my amorous feelings. But they served a purpose for me: in later life, when I found myself intimately involved in music making with the Fisherfolk, and on occasion sexually drawn to one of them, I would remember Dr. J__ and remind myself that you don't have to *act* on everything you *feel*.

My life was enriched by musical activities: joining the Galveston Music Club and playing on programs; organizing a male choir of med students, many of whom were as musical as they were medical, then making choral arrangements for them to sing. What fun! Once we did a Christmas medley including a smashing arrangement of "Jingle Bells." At home, I taught piano students in the afternoons after school. Once again I was in touch with my piano pedagogy training which had been in mothballs for a few years.

Last but not least, I had the distinct privilege of playing the little pump-organ at Canterbury House chapel where Graham held services on Sundays for medical students and staff at John Sealy. This became a challenging assignment as I neared the end of pregnancy with Nathan. With a congregation composed solely of professional medical people who could understand my dilemma and give me reassuring smiles, there I was—huffing and puffing to keep the pedals going—to produce the wheezing sounds of the organ—to accompany the congregation—whom I must also lead vocally while huffing and puffing. Is this the life we chose? Well, who knows? No wonder my Nathan turned out to be not only a doctor but a lover of hymn-singing: he was helping me pull it off *in utero*.

> *For you are my hope, O Lord God,*
> > *my confidence since I was young.*
> *I have been sustained by you ever since I was born;*
> > *from my mother's womb you have been my strength;*
> > *my praise shall be always of you.*
> > *Psalm 71: 5-6*

Ten
Motherhood

Surely the most fulfilling aspect of my life, the most challenging, the most rewarding, the most consuming: that would be motherhood. To do justice to it I should write a chapter about each of my six children. For it is they, the combined *they* in all their rich variety plus the gifted father they had, who have made me the mother I am. Their births spanned sixteen years, making the oldest an almost paternal presence to the youngest. Not only that, but the pendulum of child-rearing swung from repressive to permissive over those same sixteen years, making the younger children seem like libertines in the remembering eyes of the older.

In lieu of those six chapters, let me introduce you to the six. There is the firstborn, Bill, whom you have already met. His full name is William Graham Pulkingham III. His adult demeanor is one of dignity befitting such an impressive name, though I do believe he inherited some of that dignity from my father Leo, the judge. Bill knew the judge from boyhood—a blessing the younger children missed. Now, as a lawyer himself, he feels a kindred compassionate spirit interacting with his own, and has high regard for his grandfather's memory and reputation. There were light-hearted moments in their friendship, as on one Saturday afternoon excursion to the barbershop, when Bill was about four years old. His granddad *always* went to the barbershop on Saturday afternoons, and this one was no exception, except for the companionship of his young friend Bill, and the chance to show him off to his cronies. As they were leaving the shop walking down Main Street Bill went curiously missing. Looking around, Leo spotted him stepping off the curb and relieving himself in a nearby manhole! "Did you scold him?" my mother *Bey* wanted to know later. Leo laughed. "No indeed. I was much too impressed by his accurate aim."

Being first in line in a succession of six—though who knew *that?*—Bill had lots of photo-ops starting at an early age, and a captivating smile. "He never saw a stranger," according to Bey who took him on little excursions as a toddler. He greeted everyone he met with this dazzling smile. As he grew in stature, he grew in grace. I have family photos that show him with a protective arm around his younger brother Nathan—a gesture of care and affection. Of course, it *could* have been a restraining gesture to keep the family prankster from getting into mischief before the camera's click. Either way that big brotherly hand on the shoulder was useful. Bill was never noisy or verbose and never sought out special attention; he was—and is—a quiet strong presence in the family and a person of compassion.

Then there's Mary. Christened "Mary Graham" in honor of her paternal great-grandmother, she was our Florida sunbeam, born in the Naval Hospital at Key West where Graham had reported for duty several months before. Giving birth here was quite a switch from my earlier experience in Burlington with Bill. This maternity ward was no luxury liner. There was military precision about everything, including hitting the floor with your own two feet the morning after delivery and making your own bed—at least that's what I remember; was I delusional? The only thing this hospital had in common with Alamance General in Burlington was the absence of the baby's father on both occasions. Graham was at sea on his ship when Mary came; and Bill had been born seven weeks prematurely, making it impossible for Graham to get there in time for that great event. Thank God for *Bey*. This was back in the days when mothers of my mother's generation made themselves available to help out at times like this. After I had spent two nights in the navy hospital my mother, who was back at our little apartment taking care of Bill, was notified that it was time for me to go.

The message was simple. "Your daughter has been discharged." Since *Bey* did not drive, our downstairs neighbor Ava offered to be her chauffeur.

"As we rounded a curve and approached the hospital," Bey recounted, "my eye fell on some woman standing outside with a suitcase in her hand. And in her other arm . . . . was a *baby*.

"What? I couldn't believe my eyes. It was my own Betty Jane, standing there, holding her own suitcase *and the baby."* My mother never got over her utter amazement at that turn of events. She was still telling the story decades later. In the Navy's defense, however, I have to say that both baby Mary and I survived, and that my recovery was rapid, one could even say "with military precision."

From his ship at sea Graham wrote a letter to his very first daughter on the day of her birth. Four handwritten pages long, it begins:

Charlotte Amalie
St. Thomas
Virgin Islands
19 January 1955

Dearest Mary,

Just a word of welcome. It seems to be a habit of mine, this writing letters to my children when they first appear where I could talk to them were I only there to do it. As I did your brother Bill, I'll have to ask you to forgive my absence and realize that it's not at all intentional on my part.

One of the very first things that I want to tell you is this: that your mother is beyond doubt the sweetest most loveable person on the face of the earth. You really could not have chosen a more apt model for growing years. And incidentally, she came by her charm most naturally from the model she chose.

On the face of it, this is very flattering to me, but that is not why I include it: to me it shows how much Graham valued the gift of family and generations, and how much he wanted to reinforce the mother—daughter—grandmother relationship which Bey and Mary and I were to enjoy. Both Graham and I supported the other's parenting role and relationship to each of the children—something which became more challenging as our lives grew complex. Nonetheless we did it, never consciously undercutting one another despite sometimes sharp differences of opinion. We would work those out between us and not in front of the children. For better or for worse that's how we did it, and I think in hindsight there was more better about it than worse. The letter continues:

> *It's a curious thing, being a father. This is my second time but somehow it seems completely new and fresh. Perhaps you've noticed the slight difficulty I'm having saying things to you. I've never written to my daughter before, you know—it's a great new experience . . . Sight unseen, I'm sure you're a most handsome child—fair, dainty and sweet to all the senses . . .*

Before the letter ends he speaks to this infant girl about the importance of building a trusting relationship and confesses to her,

> *You'll think I'm a confusing person at times—contradictory and stubborn. But trust me that I'm not. My sole intention will be to present, as well as I can, the male half of the world to you in all of its worth and warmth. I must allow you to desire me but teach you not to. I must hold myself as a goal to be reached and yet foster a fierce independence of decision. While your mother will be the person you follow, I will be largely the reason you travel until someone or something moves in to take my place; and then I must love that someone or something as surely as though the choice had been*

> mine. When I fall short in these things, look at me and smile and we'll have a good laugh together . . .

He wishes her welcome and courage in this new life, and closes by saying:

> Let me tell you from the beginning that I love you most dearly and pray God that your life will be full and happy and teeming with love. Daddy.

Mary is a grand old name, as the song has it. It is a hallowed name, the name of Jesus' own mother. I sometimes think the name carries an anointing for motherhood. Certainly that's true in the case of our Mary, who, with the help of her husband John, has raised two beautiful girls to womanhood. Motherhood has been her primary commitment, involving some hard choices. And the commitment shows in the lives of those she has nurtured so lovingly. I recall making that same commitment at a point in time, but that's a story for another chapter. For now we celebrate Mary, the girl who along with her brother Bill and a handful of other white students, enrolled in Yates High School, a hitherto all-black school, in September 1969, the moment of truth for putting teeth into the new integration laws. A year later she graduated as salutatorian of her senior class. Both she and Bill stood out in the crowd, so to speak, with their long platinum blonde hair. They had a nickname for Mary at school, the other kids told me. They called her "the white Jesus." Somehow that doesn't surprise me: she has a grace and gentleness which are rare qualities in today's bustling world.

And then there's Nathan, born in Galveston, Texas, within the shadow of John Sealy Hospital, a large teaching hospital. Born when Graham was chaplain to Episcopal students and staff there, and our home was astir with gatherings of medical personnel, it is small wonder that Nathan became a doctor. From the time he was six weeks old he was rocked and cooed over by nurses and residents who were guests in our home. He was the happiest baby of the lot—always smiling, except when his diapers were changed or his face washed. His penchant for teasing showed up early on; he could literally *have me on* from the playpen by the time he was seven months old.

As he grew, other notable qualities emerged. One was how fast he could run. Another was his fiercely competitive spirit. And determination. Once, when he was four or five and we lived in Houston, I observed him shooting baskets on the basketball court at Redeemer Church. He was half the size of the high-school lads around him, but when they took a break from their practice he was there, trying to shoot a basket. Over and over he would try; Ten times, twenty times, whatever it took—*until that ball went in that basket.* "That determination will do him well," I remember thinking. To this day competitive sports and athletic expertise enthrall him. He has played soccer (all-time high scorer for his college team), racquetball (amateur champion in North Carolina one year), golf (for which his home is littered with trophies), and finally—to the utter amazement of his mother—*pool.* Here he has found *camaraderie* as a bachelor/sportsman. Sports have been Nathan's avocation, recreation, stress-reliever—well, I hope. But besides all this, he has proved himself a consummate student of the medical arts, a good off-duty diagnostician for family members, and a lover of part-singing when our family gets together and sings hymns and carols. *And . . .* he's just a lot of fun.

Jane was child Number Four—the Cuban missile crisis baby. Born on October 22, 1962, her birth-date is inextricably linked with President John Kennedy and that historic day. Being the other *middle* child in the family besides Nathan, she needed to carve out a place for herself. Actually, she was vying for a place even before she was born: there was some confusion about names, as it turned out. I *thought* we had settled on the lovely name 'Katie,' but all that changed when Graham and Nathan brought home a new pet dachshund and announced that they had named her "Katie."

"Well," I exclaimed with some indignation, "we will have to find another girl's name if we have a girl; we certainly can't name her after the *dog.*"

Once she was born, Jane proceeded to get attention in an unmistakable way—as the colic queen. For weeks lengthening into months she cried unmercifully for four hours every evening. And I, for my part, was "brought under conviction"—as our Pentecostal friends love to put it—about not breast-feeding her. "If only I had," I thought, "her tiny digestive system would have been more at peace." That is very likely true. From that time forward I determined that if God gave us another child, I would nurse the baby. Jane was the only petite child we ever had. Like a little fairy princess she was: long blonde hair in ringlets down her back, a pert expression on her face, she was altogether enchanting. She also had a mind of her own, the only one of the six who could pull a stand-off with her father about finishing her oatmeal, sitting at the table for *hours* if necessary. Finishing what was in your dish, or belonging to the "clean plate club," was a high priority for us then. This persistence on Jane's part, not the fairy-princess ambiance, would turn out to be a telling quality in her future; as a social scientist she would use her mind to great advantage and become a serious academic. Even as a young girl she was a keen observer of groups of people—waiting in train stations, and the like. She would point them out to me, commenting on their behavior towards one another as we waited for our train.

Her young life was punctuated with another near-crisis experience as we moved from suburban Austin into a changing neighborhood in Houston. Jane was nine months old. The church rectory where we lived was on a triangular block, one side of which was a heavily trafficked street with screeching sirens zooming past at all hours—within twenty feet of our bedrooms. Jane was terrified by the loud noises, and there was not much I could do to change them; I could only try to comfort her.

All six children have turned out to be sound-sensitive, which is to say musical—a combination of heredity and environment, I would say. Bill studied cello as a boy, later became an excellent guitar player, and loves choral singing. Mary graduated from university with a degree in Music Education, and quite conveniently married a music educator who had been one of her professors. Nathan loves to play guitar for relaxation, and really gets into part-singing. Jane stands out because of her beautiful solo soprano voice. Over the years she has sung in opera productions, oratorios, and in several semi-professional choirs. She also studied violin as a girl, and has recently picked it up again as a "fiddler." That leaves Martha and David, the two irrepressible and equally musical younger children.

Martha: We did not have a name selected for her when she was born; maybe I was scared off by my earlier 'Katie' experience. Somehow we were convinced she was a boy. This was before the days of testing the sex of the baby *in utero* and I'm grateful for that, since the suspense is surely part of God's game-plan—isn't it? Let's just say I liked it that way. When Graham announced her birth from the pulpit of Redeemer Church one Sunday, he simply said, "Her name is David" and after the laughter died down he went on to explain that we had been caught red-handed without a girl's name, having been so sure we had it figured out. Before she and I were released from St. Luke's Hospital her name became clear: she was to be called Martha Louise.

She would become a *big* person—not in a physical sense, though she is the tallest and strongest of the girls, and the most statuesque. No, her bigness has to do with her *persona*. When she was in her late teens she entered a room where Roland Walls, our theologian-friend from Scotland, was standing. He had not seen her since she was a young girl and exclaimed quite spontaneously, *"Martha. You're HUGE!"* I quietly reminded him that an eighteen-year-old girl might not take kindly to that description. He hastened to say, "Oh, I meant no offense, Martha. It's just that when you entered, your presence filled the entire room."

Big people are not necessarily the easiest people to live with. Take for example her father Graham, whom she resembles in so many ways. *Big* people are passionate and caring people—fervently involved with life and with those around them. They are not bystanders in any sense. Martha is that sort of person. Her father Graham was that sort of person. Martha was our first *charismatic* baby—meaning that she was born shortly after our lives were turned upside down by a new awareness of the Holy Spirit at work in our midst. Many of our friends referred to Martha as the "Hallelujah" baby. In many ways she was, and is. Martha has studied cello, played bass guitar, and loves to sing—*and* to get other people singing as well. I think she inherited the latter from me. As with Jane, her strong characteristics showed up at an early age. At the *Way In* Coffeehouse which our church ran in Houston, she would spot a loner and go crawl in that person's lap to talk to them and cheer them up. She is now a psycho-therapist.

Then there's David, the shepherd boy with a tender soul. How fitting it is that he has turned out to be the family bard, the balladeer and strummer of strings in our family and currently the only professional musician. He too was born on "renewal row" during a period of intense spiritual activity at and around our church in Houston. His love of people manifested early, as he attended his own baby shower at the age of three weeks. That was due to his being born a month early, taking advantage of the *free baby* offer at a new hospital. It was a time like that, when well-nigh unbelievable things were happening almost daily.

David was a winsome child, with big blue eyes that could melt your heart straightaway. As he grew in stature, so he did in insight and understanding—almost as if he had been here before and already knew some things. He was always *present* to the moment and the people he was with, a quality he never lost—even through the rigors of adolescence. Once, when he was fifteen and in boarding-school in Florida, I made a long-distance phone call to him, having been overseas for some period of time. The only place David could take the call was in a crowded hallway with his teenage contemporaries all around. He seemed oblivious to them, and all about me. When he recognized my voice he exclaimed, "Mom! Mom, is that really you? Mom, I love you *so much.*" In reflecting on this moment, I had to wonder how many teenage boys would have been that free to show such affection to their mother, with their contemporaries within earshot. Not many, that's my guess.

Graham, the father of this wonderful brood, taught our children much about loving. He said in a sermon once, "Love is something you are *doing.*" He lived his life that way. One night, several years after his death, I wrote this letter to him in my personal journal:

Saturday, March 6

Dear Graham,

Tonight I was so aware of you, so thankful to you for all the guidance and direction and inspiration you gave our children. People frequently marvel at our children: their diversity, their accomplishments, their "doing well." But of course, they are only doing what you always told them—do well. It was your final word to them on many occasions, after many visits: "Do well." You constantly called them to excellence, to be the best that they possibly could be. It was both a great challenge and a freeing moment. You did not say, "Be like me," or "Imitate your mother." You said "Do well," and in so saying you threw out a challenge with vast possibilities, but one that could only be defined by the person doing the well-doing."

Graham was also fond of saying, "And don't forget to say a good word for Jesus."

I have taken you way ahead of myself chronologically by describing each of these six wonderful children, and commenting on their father's legacy. We must do a little back tracking to see how all of these pieces fit together

Children are a heritage from the Lord,
 and the fruit of the womb is a gift.
Like arrows in the hand of a warrior
 are the children of one's youth.
Happy is the man who has his quiver full of them!
 Psalm 127: 4-6a

The Knott family in 1903. Bey and Jane are the little girls in white. Note 3 brothers with musical instruments on far right.

Bey and Leo and the Model-T Ford, 1920

Leo with daughter Betty Jane in 1934,
the year she started to school

Betty at her WCUNC senior piano recital, May 13, 1949

Betty and Graham sing Christmas carols with friends in Austin, Texas, 1950

On Bey's front lawn in N.C., Summer 1951

The Six Pulkingham Children, Houston, Texas, 1969. (Front row: Martha, Jane, Nathan. Back row: Mary, Bill, holding David)

Redeemer Church,
Houston, Texas

Yeldall Manor,
Berkshire, England

Cathedral of the Isles,
Isle of Cumbrae, Scotland

Chapel of the Holy Spirit,
Community of Celebration,
Aliquippa, Pennsylvania

Betty directs Church of Redeemer Choir,
Mimi and Conway accompanying, 1970

This is how you sing "Ah . . ."

The Fisherfolk tour in the UK, 1984

Graham in his clerical garb, circa 1986

Bey and Jane at home in 1993

Herb Wendell, David Williams, Rose Anne Gant and Betty, October 9, 1996

Betty holding twins Ella and Graham at their baptism at St. James Episcopal Church in Austin, TX. Christening dress worn by all six Pulkinghams is worn here by Ella (the dress) and Graham (the slip, topped with a jacket)—an idea their grandmother concocted. January, 2008

Eleven

Transitions

Sometimes people ask, "How on earth did you manage to take care of *six children?*" I answer blithely,

"Oh, we started a community, so I would have some help." That comment usually gets a laugh, and gets *me* off the hook of trying to explain something fairly unexplainable. The truth is, our large progeny was not the motivation for community, but our extended household in the sixties was a big help to me personally.

Before any of that happened came Graham's apprenticeship in parish ministry: accepting a call as Associate Rector to Charles Sumners, rector of St. David's, Austin. By 1960 Graham had been on the domestic mission field for three years and was ready to broaden his experience. This was the perfect place to do it: in an established—indeed, historic for Texas—downtown church with a kindly rector and an incredibly hospitable wife. Charles and Virginia Sumners were so good to us, so good *for* us. Truly gracious and welcoming and loving people they were. I can't imagine either of us could have had better role models.

So three more years went by in a flash. We were both fully occupied—Graham with the Christian education program of the parish and I with the home front which now included two school-aged children, one pre-schooler and baby Jane. Needless to say, music was on the back burner for me though I managed to sing in the church choir, which prevented total withdrawal symptoms. Baby Jane had finally outgrown the colic and was blossoming into a beautiful young lass.

Bill and Mary were fortunate to attend St. Andrews Episcopal School, where our good friend Lillian Corner—of laundry fame—taught. They enjoyed other upper-middle-class pleasures like ballet lessons for Mary, judo class for Bill. Though our income was meager as compared with that of our neighbors, we were able to partake of many suburban advantages. I guess you could call them *clergy perks*, otherwise known as *knowing the right people*. Bill studied cello, managing to break the necks of only two instruments as he clambered out of the car and up a hill for lessons. He sang the young lad's role in a University of Texas production of Puccini's Gianni Schicchi when he was eleven. Mary's gifts were delightfully domestic—thank goodness. She always knew where I had left the scissors or the shopping list, she was a great help with the younger children, and have I thanked you enough, Lord, for sending such a child at such a moment in my life?

Nathan was only three-and-a-half when invited to participate in the U.T. Laboratory Nursery School program for a couple of half-days each week. This was not due to any great merit of his own, though he might beg to differ were he telling this tale, but because the director of the program was a member of St. David's and wanted to make this available to us. As soon as he was deposited at the door of the nursery school, Nathan would make a beeline for the puzzle section. He loved solving puzzles as a small boy; and as a pathologist he is *still* solving problems today. When psychiatrist friends from the old days in Galveston dropped by for visits, Nathan challenged them to a game of Concentration, the card-game based on visual memory skills. They would humor him by agreeing to play, then get the socks beat off of them—initially because they were bantering with other adults while engaging in this *child's play*; but then, even when they buckled down and tried their hardest, he *still* beat them. This early memory-gift was a precursor of his astounding recall of medical facts today. Nathan says it's in the D.N.A. from his grandmother Bey who had a prodigious capacity for memorization. Family members have learned not to ask Nathan a casual medical question—unless they are prepared for encyclopedic answers, sparing no detail.

Under Graham's leadership, Christian education at St. David's flourished. Following the family service on Sunday mornings, there was an "unpacking the sermon" session for adults—right there in the nave of the church. Question and answer sessions were Graham's forte, and these were dynamic sessions for all who attended. A Sunday evening youth program designed by Graham and his capable Christian Education assistant Virginia Withey whom he hired to help him—for the well-nigh unbelievable amount of *ten dollars a week*—involved junior and senior high students and included a meal and classes for each age-group. I volunteered to teach one of the classes, a group of twelve seventh graders including the rector's son. My teaching assistant was a local seminarian. We studied the four gospels, and I loved the challenge of preparing for these classes. The youth had reading assignments week by week, and really *did them;* they were great kids. It was an unforgettable and very positive experience for me. As for Virginia's involvement, little did any of us know that our earlier acquaintance with her at Canterbury House and our present involvement at St. David's would be but a prelude to a lifelong friendship and many shared adventures.

Enter Bishop John Hines: *yet again.* This bishop functioned like the hound of heaven with his clergy. He knew their strengths and when to beckon them to higher ground. So it was, at least, with Graham. He had discerned Graham's passion for the church in the city. Now he wanted him to consider a call to be rector of Church of the Redeemer in Houston. Urban churches faced complex problems: there were changing demographics, for one thing. There was mounting racial tension throughout the land. There were new suburbs luring upper-middle-class families to a cleaner, calmer surround for their family life, leaving inner-city churches bereft of numbers both in membership and money. Houston's Church of the Redeemer fit that description. The retiring rector had been there for eighteen years, and older members of the parish felt like "retiring" with him from the uncertainties of the changing neighborhood around them.

Eastwood had been Houston's first residential development east of the industrial and commercial core of the city. Begun circa 1916 by a developer named William Wilson, it had all the earmarks of becoming a stable community sure to attract families, and it did. Wilson was very likely an Episcopalian, since he gave to the Episcopal Church a triangular block set aside for a church to serve Eastwood. It was appropriately called "Eastwood Community Church."

From the outset, due to the initiative of then Episcopal Bishop of Texas, Clinton S. Quin, the church had an Episcopal priest as its minister, the first being Valentine Lee from Virginia. The Episcopal label was not pushed in any way, so much so that many members of the church were not even aware of their minister's denominational stripes. It was clearly the hope of the bishop *and* the developer that they were planting a church which would serve the needs of the entire growing community. That little gleaning, unearthed from the chronology of this neighborhood and this church's origins, speaks volumes to me about what developed there, in more ways than real estate.

It was to such a church in such a neighborhood that we were called in 1963. Before the call came officially we had visited the church one weekend and Graham had preached at the Sunday service. Before that I had asked a million questions, trying as best I could to ascertain what this church and neighborhood would be like for us if we moved there. Graham had already been there and scoped out the neighborhood, so I asked him,

"Well, what does the church *look like*—I mean, architecturally?" He pondered for a moment and said,

"I guess you would call it *Modern Theatrical.*"

What's that? I wondered. Seeing my puzzled look, he went on to explain, "It's like nothing you've ever seen before. There are no windows." In this respect it was certainly like a theater. "There are no right angles anywhere. The whole structure is poured concrete, and curving lines are the norm. The lighting is indirect, coming from large neon tubing overhead. And then there's this mural that functions as a reredos: it covers the entire wall behind the altar."[2] I could tell he was intrigued by what he had seen.

Well, I was both intrigued and mystified by his description. It was certainly unlike any Episcopal church I had ever seen. When we arrived for the weekend in question, sure enough—everything was different, just as Graham had said. Entering through large glass doors from Telephone Road, the narthex was spacious with tile flooring, and the ushers handed out orders of service in the manner of programs at a theater. Proceeding into the nave was like entering a cave: it was dark in here. I wondered how people managed to read the orders of service. The floor was graded gently downward, like most good theaters, aiding visibility for those seated towards the back. Once the narthex doors had been closed we were in a virtually soundproof interior.

When my eyes became accustomed to the dim lighting, I was suddenly transfixed by the remarkable mural beyond the altar, as I might have been by a dazzling scene on a wide cinema screen. Light was streaming from this painting depicting Christ's *parousia,* his coming again in glory. His right hand is raised in a gesture of welcome, his left hand extended as though bestowing a gift. Beneath him stand contemporary working men and women gazing up—some with caps respectfully in hand. They seem awestruck.

I was awestruck too. The whole experience was surreal, unlike anything I'd seen before. The acolytes who lit the candles before the service emerged from behind a bush—no, that can't be true, it was a concealed door that *looked* like a bush. The sacristy door was part of the landscape-depicting mural. Over it all the ceiling was smoky-blue and unmistakably sky-ish. When the Eucharistic celebration began, the ranks of acolytes grew to a sizeable drill-team moving about the sanctuary with military

---

2   See Cover photo of mural, taken by Tom Milner on February 27, 2011.

precision, through ritualized behaviors and postures they had been taught. My jaw dropped in amazement several times as I "watched the show." For that is surely what it was: whatever else was of its essence, it *was* a good show. By contrast stood the small choir, led by four professional soloists. There were several volunteer members in the choir, but they seemed inconsequential since the only identifiable sounds came from the four powerful, unblended voices.

Meanwhile, out in the pews I was struggling to read the hymnal numbers in the order of service. The neon lights had dimmed gradually over the years, so gradually that no one seemed to notice. If they had, the matter had gone untended. Not surprisingly, congregational participation in the liturgy was minimal, the responses barely audible. Attendance was spotty, the people scattered over the fairly large nave of the church. "Oh, dear," I might well have thought. But the Holy Spirit was way out ahead of me with a much bolder proclamation of the moment. From the depths of my being, in a near-audible voice came the words:

Let everything that hath breath praise the Lord!"

Everything inside of me wanted to jump up and shout, "Yes, yes!" Because in that moment I could imagine a church filled with praise in this self-same spot, a singing church, a praising church. God had spoken. I had heard the word.

The move to Houston was not like being "carried to the skies on flowery beds of ease," as the hymn-writer has it. No move is easy. This one was hard on several levels: The rectory was still full of workmen completing the conversion of the carport into a family room—something Graham and I had insisted on for our growing family. The hardest part was the major adjustment for the children—from an advantaged neighborhood in Austin to a seriously disadvantaged one in Houston. Ten-year-old Bill cried every morning before going to school—for weeks on end. I thought his grief would end in a day or two, but no.

Encouraging him to pick up his school-bag and get going felt to me like sweeping him out of the house. It was so painful—for us both.

Then there was dear old Mr. Tom Telepsen, the head of Telepsen Construction Company and influential member of the church. His vision had put this church on the map—in more ways than one. First off, during the Great Depression years he had kept his construction crews working and eating by paying them out of his own pocket. They built the gymnasium attached to the education building of the church. Having come to the USA as a Norwegian immigrant, he had great empathy for the workingman's plight. He also had been the visionary for the pace-setting poured concrete structure of the new church building in the fifties. And that was not all. When another Norwegian immigrant came to him looking for work as a painter, Mr. Tom's response had been swift. Taking him to his own home, he had showed him the dining room which needed painting. Returning at day's end, he was totally surprised by what he found. John William Orth had painted a beautiful mural on one of the dining room walls.

"Oh," Telepsen exclaimed. "So *that's* the kind of painter you are."

He told Orth about a recurring dream of Christ he had had recently, and asked him, "Do you think you could paint *that?*" Orth assured him that he could, and the rest is history and explains the mural that still—to this day—stops people dead in their tracks when they enter the worship space at Redeemer Church.

Now Mr. Tom, officially retired, was personally supervising the conversion of the rectory garage into our new family room. With these other big projects under his belt, this must have seemed like child's play, or like going from the sublime to the ridiculous—I'm not sure which. The proposed room was predictably the length of the former garage, with a utility room built across the back. The only window in the entire space was an ordinary-sized window on the front towards Dallas Avenue.

"Mr. Tom," I exclaimed. "Can't we make it a double window, or a big picture window?"

"Why"—pronounced *Fye* in his Norwegian accent—"do you need more windows? In the vinter you haf the heat, in the summer you haf the air-conditioning."

"But . . . we need more *light* in this big room," I pleaded.

We talked, I stuck to my guns, and praise be to God. We did get a big picture window that shed light in the room. Thank you, Mr. Tom. Perhaps this little cultural interchange was to prepare me for many challenges to come—accustoming the ear to a variety of Anglo-Saxon accents ranging from the King's English to Glaswegian Scottish—not to be confused with English—to the South African, Aussie and Kiwi varieties. For that is where our travels would take us: all over the English-speaking world. Oh, my: How different the language and vocabulary-of-choice could be.

As the dust settled from the construction project, more dust began to rise from the *real* business at hand: meeting the challenge of facing the future. The church we had chosen to serve had a bleak prognosis demographically. Population wedges of Hispanics and Afro-Americans were edging their way towards this once-stable, once-settled Anglo neighborhood. Some older members had already transferred their letters to suburban churches. Their only compelling reason to remain had been their loyalty to the retiring rector. Now that he had departed, they were ready to depart as well. Things were changing around them.

Things were changing in my world, too. Directly across the street from the church was Lantrip Elementary School, named for its first principal Dora Lantrip. Her friend Shirley Carlisle, a charter member of Redeemer, had cooked and served the first hot soup for students there in the early pre-1920 days. Now in the sixties, I agreed to serve as an officer in the P.T.A. One of the issues was the overcrowded condition in un-air-conditioned classrooms. Perhaps one has to live in Texas to appreciate the fact that "summer" can begin in April and last until November. The fact that children—including my own—were crammed into these stuffy, miserable rooms and expected not only to behave, but to study and learn, disturbed me greatly. So I began contacting. H. I. S. D., the local school district office, to inquire into this situation, because I knew very well that there were schools in other parts of the city that *did* have air-conditioning. The bottom-line answer I got was this: kids in the East End aren't accustomed to air-conditioning at home, so they won't miss it at school. Never mind that at home *none* of them lived in a poorly ventilated room with forty other warm bodies. The school system's response infuriated me, but there was no quick fix, I knew. Some of society's inequities were becoming up-close and personal.

Still, all of this was just the precursor of things to come. Our first year living in a changing neighborhood in Houston was a year of major adjustment for us all—from the oldest to the youngest. Even Nathan, the one who was usually so gung-ho and confident, seem puzzled by the move. Riding his tricycle round and round the triangular block covered by the church and the rectory, he came in one day and said, "Mama, how can my friends come over?" Good question. No quick answers.

Here we were on a little island surrounded by a moat of heavily trafficked city streets. Filling the companionship gap temporarily was Olin, the church sexton and *only* full-time employee besides the rector. Nathan would hang out with Olin, consuming case-loads of *pop* until we discovered that and reined in the habit. Mary, I am sure, felt the loss of things like ballet classes and the advantages that had come our way in Austin; but she didn't seem to take the move as hard as Bill. That was fortunate for me; had she done so we *all* might have ended up in a pool of tears at the end of the school day.

Graham was well aware that I had my hands full helping our four children through this big time of adjustment; consequently, he spared me some of his own agony—which was considerable. Had I known the depths of his despair over the situation, I could have been more empathetic . . . *maybe*. But somehow I doubt it; I was too full of my own burdens, too self-concerned.

Graham had come to Redeemer full of high hopes for reviving a church in demise; it was right along the lines of the social gospel teaching that had been front and center at seminary. He came with lots of ideas for creative ministries in a neighborhood like this. Perceiving how many aimless youths were wandering the streets, most of them drop-outs from high school, he did a couple of things. With the help of a young postulant to Holy Orders who needed hands-on ministry experience to test his own vocation, Graham took over the management of a gas station in the neighborhood, one that was threatening to fold. The idea here was to give some gainful employment and on-the-job training to some of these youths. Another project was opening the church gymnasium to the neighborhood. Unfortunately, Graham turned out to be the sole custodian of that project most of the time, and unruly behavior became an increasing problem. It wasn't long before the kids had virtually trashed the gym and it had to be closed and the project discontinued. The gas station fared no better—undependable workers, mishandling of monies: this wasn't working either.

"I tried everything they taught me in seminary, and none of it worked," Graham commented in later years.

It was with a great sense of relief that we made it through 'til the summer of 1964, when we headed for North Carolina on a two-week family holiday and visit with my family. Once there for only a few days Graham shared with me that the Lord had told him to go to New York. Now *there's* a great idea for a family holiday, thought I. *Fine*. We'll see you around—*if the Lord wills*. I was so angry. Graham was in hopes of seeing David Wilkinson, the renowned Assembly of God minister whose book *The Cross and the Switchblade* both of us had read that spring. Mixed in with my resentment about our family holiday turning into his personal pilgrimage—or whatever it was—was a secret longing that I too might be set free from my years-long addiction to cigarettes. After all, Wilkinson was helping people get free of heroin, cocaine and all manner of drugs. Why couldn't I stop smoking?

While he was gone on this New York jaunt, I had time to do a lot of thinking. I told my mother Bey that I was worried about Graham's mental state. His behavior had been increasingly erratic, it seemed to me. He had begun to seek out people outside of the Redeemer fellowship: nothing wrong with that, except I didn't really know them myself, though I knew they were people of faith in other denominations. Looking back, this was much more of a reflection of my own fears than of anything to do with Graham. He had likely met them through Grace Murray, a saintly and prayerful woman at Redeemer—the one to whom God had "spoken" saying Graham was to be the new rector. When that happened, Graham had retorted in his typical cocky way, "Well, I hope God remembers to tell the vestry too." Well, God had, and now here we were in something of a jumble. I told Bey I just didn't know how much longer I could hold on—meaning to my sanity, or to a sense that we were really headed in the right direction.

She told *me*—get this now—"not to touch the Lord's anointed." She pulled that out of the Bible somewhere, as she could so aptly do when the occasion seemed to demand. This was the mother who had excelled in Biblical studies at the Baptist Seminary in Louisville; there were no flies on her when it came to quoting the Bible accurately—and appropriately. If I were looking for a shoulder to cry on, clearly I would have to look elsewhere; my good Baptist mother was not supplying it. Yet, she could not have been kinder to me and to the children; she was just not buying my interpretation of the situation. Thank goodness. My interpretation was at this point very skewed, very frightened, and not something to hang your hat on. Had she not stiffened my spine with this reminder that God, after all, might *just* be in charge here, since it was the same God who had called us to serve at Redeemer, I might never have gone back to Houston.

Unbeknownst to me until later, this trip had been preceded by Graham's spending hours lengthening into days in Redeemer Church's little basement chapel, weeping and praying to the Lord. "Lord," he had said, "if you want this church to die, I will help you bury it. If you want it to live, help me . . ."

When the opportunity came to meet David Wilkerson in New York, he had been prepared to go for it. Now, by that remarkable gift called hindsight, I can see what a stellar opportunity this was for Graham, how strategic to all that lay ahead. But I didn't see it then. I was—in soul miles—*light-years* away from being ready for this. Graham knew this; and somehow must have known, which is to say *trusted,* that the Lord would get me on board by and by. He was right. By and by, but it was a journey.

I was vastly relieved when Graham returned safely from New York. After all, he had left with only a few dollars in his pocket, saying, "The Lord will provide." That's how convinced he was that he was on God's mission. And he was. At the time it seemed crazy. Crazy. Crazy. My good Methodist father, raised by Scots Presbyterian grandparents, had been taught to "look down the road" and make provision for the future. This behavior was nowhere on his radar screen, yet he was a godly man. Only my mother—a woman of extraordinary faith—stood in the breach. I wouldn't have made it through without her.

One aspect of God's provision for the journey had to do with Lillian Corner. Once Graham had reached New York and made arrangements to see David Wilkerson the next day, he had some time on his hands, but—alas—no money. Suddenly he remembered that Lillian often went in the summer to visit family in New Jersey, not far from "the city." In yet another miracle of circumstance, Lillian *just happened* to be there visiting and welcomed Graham with open arms—and fed him, too. All of this was comforting information to me. Yet our homecoming to Houston felt like returning to prison after an approved leave of absence. It felt that way to *me*. Certainly not to Graham, who was flying high as a kite.

> *Hear my cry, O God,*
>   *and listen to my prayer.*
> *I call upon you from the ends of the earth*
>   *with heaviness in my heart:*
>   *set me upon the rock that is higher than I.*
>   *Psalm 61: 1-2*

Twelve
MY LIFE GOES . . . TILT!

Life definitely goes in a new direction from this point on. Whatever happened to Graham in New York will affect the rest of us for sure. What is not clear at this point is *how?* He has come home with a new gleam in his eye, and I have come home to—*what?* A prison? That's how it had been feeling for so long. I could identify with that little boy on the tricycle circling the block and asking, "How can my friends come over?" The retiring rector's wife's assurance that *no one will bother you here* haunted me. I recall that it had sent a chill down my spine when she said it, and that's before we moved into the rectory and *experienced* it.

Not that I had been idle. Unlike the elderly wife of the retiring rector, I had been extremely busy with kids and new schools and diapers and all the rest of it. But where was the fellowship, the camaraderie, the koinonia, of Christianity? Also, my life had suddenly been stripped of all the comforts of suburbia, the easy socializing skills of affluent Episcopalians—so sophisticated and self-assured. These I had left behind in Austin. And now, here we were. Where was the joy?

Well, it was waiting for me. But first I had to walk through a maze. I had to allow my life to be tipped over like a box being emptied of its contents and re-constituted. There's no other way to describe it. Suddenly, people seemed to be everywhere. And they were not *regular* Episcopal-type people as I had known them. No two of them were alike:

There was a Greek-American charismatic layman who always attended the Tuesday night meetings Graham had started. He was lively, knew different songs, marched to a different drumbeat than I was used to, but clearly loved the same Lord.

There were prayer-and-praise meetings including Bible teaching, something we had never done before but which Graham had been encouraged to start. Perhaps they would help channel the tremendous new energy all around us so we could find out what God intended to *do* with it.

There was Grace Murray, the saintly woman from Redeemer who had prayed her heart out that God would do *something* to renew this church. She was in seventh heaven now that things were on the move.

There were others—some from the parish and some from across town who were spirit-led people—*whatever that meant.* I wasn't entirely sure, and some days I was reminded of what Charles Sumners had said about the godly but overly enthused women in his flock: "I don't know if they have something I don't have, or something I don't want." What I did know was that I was on a moving escalator which was headed somewhere I had never been before.

There were days when I wanted to run away. The farthest place I ever ran was to the upstairs attic in the rectory where I hid one day in total despair—it was all just too much. I will never forget that day: how scared I felt, how overwhelmed, as I sat there amidst boxes and Christmas decorations and out-of-season clothes. I don't know how long I had been there—an hour perhaps—when up the steps came the hound-of-heaven, my own husband Graham, to find me. Like a shepherd looking for a lost sheep, he found me huddled in a corner, brooding over life's impossibilities. He was so gentle; he was so kind. He did not once condemn me or upbraid me for my behavior. He simply sought me out, was there with me, and somehow I felt befriended and consoled. The Good Shepherd had sent one of his assistant shepherds to rescue me—just when I needed rescuing.

My own struggles to stop smoking continued—a kind of smokescreen covering great *angst* of soul and much travail. Only after I had witnessed several incidences of the Lord's power to heal instantaneously—only then was I ready to move ahead and embrace what the Spirit was offering. One incident happened at the altar rail of our church when a woman on crutches left the altar *without them*. I had never seen anything like this before. The other happened when the warts on my hands disappeared overnight; it turned out that Graham had awakened that very night with a sense that he was to lay hands on me and pray. He did, and the warts were no more. On the following Sunday evening we found ourselves once again at Grace Chapel, the little Chinese-American church we had been visiting during the autumn. This time I was more than ready for whatever the Lord was offering. As Graham retells it:

"There among the gentle and self-effacing oriental Christians, Betty received her own baptism of power. It was for me an experience of the most exquisite beauty. Sitting beside Betty was a young girl of about eighteen, and standing nearby were three or four of the Chinese women talking to the pastor's wife . . . Most of the congregation had already dispersed, and Betty was waiting for her turn for the elder's prayers. Suddenly she stood up, transfigured, with her eyes closed and her hands extended heavenward in a graceful attitude of supplication. Then to my amazement she opened her mouth and began what sounded like an operatic love song in a language I had never heard before. As she did this, the girl beside her arose and, laying one hand gently on Betty's shoulder, began a perfect contrapuntal melody, the two sang a duet in the Spirit. Then the women joined in a chorus in several different tongues, and for perhaps two or three minutes the most angelic sounds I have ever heard filled the small chapel." The Lord had met me in a new and empowering way; I felt washed clean, filled with a new peace and joy, and ready for what lay ahead.

So much was happening so fast that I can't possibly say just when what happened *happened*. I only know *that* it happened.

When your life is turned upside down and everything seems topsy-turvy, that's just the way it is. There wasn't time to keep a diary. There were many new faces showing up for services, especially for the Tuesday evening gathering which met in a large room in the education wing of the church. There were people turning up at odd hours for a multitude of reasons. I recall one fellow who seemed to have come from nowhere, and was zealous with a loose screw in the mix somewhere; he literally "came to church" one day by driving his truck right across the rectory sidewalk and almost up to the front door. For the life of me I can't remember whether his brakes failed or the screw was loose that day.

Then there was the couple whom God had told to sell what they had and give to the poor. They moved out of their home, put a lot of their "stuff" on the sidewalk outside the rectory, their interpretation of the easiest way to give to the poor. They then ended up on our doorstep fully expecting to be cared for, because after all we were spirit-led Christians, they had been told. We *did* take them in for several weeks until some suitable direction had been established for them as a family. How grateful I was for Bob Eckert, our doctor-friend from Galveston days, who had emerged again in our lives and was on hand with his own word from the Lord concerning the newcomers in our household. "I remember St. Paul told some of the early Christians that those who don't work don't get to eat." *How timely.* I felt grateful for the reminder that those early Christians had developed some practical sense in ordering their daily lives. Perhaps their example could help *us* now.

The good doctor was not the only dedicated layperson who showed up—quite literally—to help, to pray, to be of service. There was also Jerry Barker, a respected lawyer from Galveston. Both these men moved their families into our depressed neighborhood. In nearby Pasadena an ardent Methodist, Ladd Fields, was awakened in the night with the name *Church of the Redeemer* on his mind, and the sense that God wanted him to *go there.* The new spiritual energies emerging attracted the attention of a welder and Methodist lay-preacher named Grover Newman who had driven past Redeemer for years and considered it off his radar screen. John Grimmet was a member of the church and a lineman with Houston Light & Power when he felt *pulled in* by the net God seemed to be casting all around the area. God was looking for laborers in His vineyard. These men of faith and their wives and families helped stabilize what was going on, else we might have found ourselves awash in a sea of confusion. But they *did come,* bringing with them extraordinary gifts of leadership. They had caught Graham's vision of renewing the church right here in the heart of Houston's East End.

It would be easy, at this point, to look back and laugh at *all of us*—those who might be termed the "crazies" who came our way, and ourselves for being so open. It was really Pandora's Box that had been opened. We had been praying for a release of the spirit, for new answers in a situation where packaged institutional answers were not working. Here it all was, exploding around us. We had not yet had much experience in what it means to *discern the spirits*, the kind of thing St. Paul encountered in Acts 16 with the slave girl who had a gift of divination, but clearly *not* from the Holy Spirit. We had much to learn. There were genuinely humorous moments, but this I know: God the Spirit was at work in the mayhem, refashioning our lives into useful servanthood; and the "crazies?" They were all people on a quest, and in that sense no different than we. Very early on we learned to ask the Lord to send *just* the people He hand-picked to us; then, having prayed *believing* God would do just that, we were free to welcome everyone as a heaven-sent visitor, a person here for God's purposes. Had we not learned to pray this way, we might easily have taken refuge in a social-service mentality, set up quotas we could deal with and other protective mechanisms. Instead, we counted on God to protect us.

The Lord sent some interesting visitors-cum-ministers our way; they were a colorful part of Pandora's Box. We didn't go *looking* for these people; they came looking for us, having heard about the Spirit's moving in our midst. There were fiery tongue-speaking evangelists, there were free-church ministers from Britain, and of course Brother Earle Frid, with his Canadian Baptist background, who took us by the hand and led us into studying the Bible as the most exciting book in the world. He was more than a visitor, and became a regular teacher at mid-week Bible studies and services, a most unaccustomed thing in most Episcopal churches. His only objection to me, he told one of the church members, was that I wore too much rouge on my face. That was odd, since I had never touched the stuff. But it did show me that even ministers who know a lot about some things can be wrong about others. Another noteworthy visitor was Michael Harper, an Anglican priest who was very involved with Fountain Trust in England, an organization borne of the renewal movement there. Michael and his wife Jeanne became very important links to the U.K. as things developed.

To make life even more interesting and complicated, I was pregnant again. Back in Austin I had had recurring back problems, days when I could hardly crawl out of bed because of severe muscle spasms. I had even been hospitalized and placed on a regimen of complete bed rest and muscle relaxing medications. That had helped, but the problem was not solved, and followed me to Houston, surfacing again during our first stress-ridden year in the East End.

Graham said, "Let's go see Dr. Ainsworth. He is an excellent orthopedic surgeon." Off we went, taking advantage of one of the medical connections Graham had made during Galveston days. The surgeon's tests were thorough and his findings unequivocal. "You have a degenerative disc in your lower back—likely due to some accident earlier in your life. Your lower spine looks very much like the spine of a ninety-year-old woman."

Sure enough, as we talked I clearly remembered falling down a marble staircase as I was leaving my piano lesson in the Alamance Hotel, turning two somersaults on the way down and leaving my teacher Dr. Moore with an ashen countenance as he gazed down at me. I would have been about eleven at the time. "That would do it," Dr. Ainsworth said. He prescribed a course of physical therapy, exercises to do at home, and said before we left, "Of course, you should avoid becoming pregnant." *Right*. With four beautiful children at home, that didn't sound especially punitive; still, there had been this sense that God was not finished with the quiver-full of children intended for us.

So now, I *was* pregnant and we would just have to deal with the back problem. Actually, the Lord dealt with the back problem, and in a most remarkable way: my back was healed miraculously through the laying on of hands and the prayers of God's people at that same little Chinese-American church. How I got *to* the front of that church for prayer was equally remarkable. One of the church elders shared a dream he had had the previous night: a vision of a brand new spinal cord, healthy and whole. At the close of the service, when people were invited to come forward for healing prayers, I managed not to trample anyone in my haste to get there before they gave that new spine to anyone else. *That* is how convinced, how totally sure I was that *that was my new spine.* And it was. The difference it made in my life—immediately—was phenomenal. No wonder Martha, with whom I was pregnant at the time, became known as the "Hallelujah" baby. God was at work in wondrous ways while she was in *utero.*

Change was happening all around—in people's lives individually, and in the structure of our family households. Three young adults were now fully a part of our rectory household. They were Nancy Carr, a string music teacher who happened to be my sister, Arabella Miner, a lifelong Episcopalian now working at Houston's famed medical center, and Bill Farra, a recently widowed young lawyer. All three had caught the fresh new vision of *being* the church here on the corner of Telephone Road and Dallas Avenue in Houston. That was the vision that Graham had, and by the Spirit's empowering gifts he was able to communicate that vision to many others. Living under the same roof, sharing the same meals as well as a sense of responsibility for the unique ministry of the ordained minister's household: these were the things these three dedicated young adults bought into. It was not by fiat that it happened; it was a process.

Bill came to us as a grieving young widower who had lost his wife of four months to leukemia. He also came bearing a gift we badly needed: a church organist. I had been pinch-hitting in this role for a brief time, and only—I told the Lord—*until* the person He had chosen for the job turned up. One day Graham brought Bill into the church where I was dutifully trying to learn the hymns for Sunday and simplify the pedal parts. When he introduced me to Bill Farra and *just happened* to mention that he was an organist, I thought I had seen an angel. I still think that. No one has ever or more clearly been sent into my life than this wonderful friend named Bill.

Arabella came with a heart-hunger for God, and a determination to set out on the pilgrim's way: to track the steps of Jesus during this earthly life-span, to make her life count. I wonder now whether some of that zeal to get going *now* and just *do it* was the result of having worked at M.D. Anderson Cancer Hospital amidst so many terminal cases and premature deaths. Whatever its source, her zeal was a clear and present gift. She also had lots of maternal wisdom, albeit not yet a mother. She could have published a book called "My mother always said . . ." Her mother knew the fine art of giving babies in high chairs cobs of cooked corn all de-kerneled and buttered—a strategy for keeping children quiet at the table for a *long* time, while they sucked the goodness out of that corn cob. Arabella's mother was oft-quoted and oft-heeded at the rectory. Arabella herself fitted in seamlessly as a nanny with our children—especially the younger three. This freed me to spend more time at the church doing my *music thing*.

My sister Nancy was the only one of the three who maintained a full-time job outside the home. She headed up the string music program in the Deer Park Schools southeast of Houston and not far from N.A.S.A. As a bread-winner for the household she helped support the other lay-ministers now fully occupied at the church, Bill and Arabella. She was also a great musician herself and loved to sing. *All* of us participated in the Redeemer choir. Nancy and Arabella single-handedly—which is to say *double-handedly*—built up the outdated anthem library of the choir.

This little picture of how our household came to be extended is a microcosm of what happened across the landscape at Redeemer Church during the mid-sixties. Once the concept of household *ministry* took hold—the concept that each household *has* a ministry and is part of the ministering Body of Christ in this place, many households began to expand to accommodate the new vision. Of course, none of it would have happened unless the rector's household went first. Ours was the vision-setting household of necessity, since the sheep cannot venture where the shepherd has not led them.

Now that my life had gone *full-tilt,* anything could happen—and most of it *did.* We were no longer a typical middle-class American family; we were—for want of a better term—an experiment in community living. Some would call it what has become a pejorative word: a *commune;* but we were not an opting-out-of-society group fenced in by strict rules and closed doors to the world around us. We were an active Episcopal parish in good standing in the Diocese of Texas. And we were trying new things to see if the church of Jesus Christ, a church we loved, could actually *work* in the urban jungle of a city like Houston. We believed it could, but only as we expanded our concept of what a family might look like in a place like this. We *wanted* it to work, and we knew there were personal sacrifices we would need to make along the way. We were willing to take some risks for the Gospel's sake, to see what the Lord might do with the likes of us.

For my brethren and companions' sake,
I pray for your prosperity.
Because of the house of the Lord our God,
I will seek to do you good.
Psalm 122: 8-9

Thirteen
Music Wherever She Goes . . .

Once your life goes *tilt,* you're on a voyage and you feel the waters moving beneath you. You are no longer land-locked. Life lacks a certain predictability it once had. It has instead the quality of a daily adventure. In the past I had relied on long hand-written lists to order my days and accomplish things that needed doing. Now the Lord was urging me to take a chance on spontaneity in my well-ordered life, to trust that inner voice, those urgings of the spirit, to "let go and let God" as someone famously said.

So, from this point on, my remembrances will be less chronological than intuitional. I have never been an astute chronicler of events and won't try to be one now. Much of my own journey can best be described as a song, a journey of the soul.

For as long as I can remember I have loved singing together with people and hearing people sing together. Starting back in fourth grade class when Mrs. Charles taught us to sing in parts—and I couldn't *wait* to get home and try out the latest parts on Bey and Jane—then continuing with high-school glee club, college chorus, and church choirs everywhere I lived, it was true: *she shall have music wherever she goes.* That is the magic of music—that you can find it, or make it happen *anywhere and everywhere.*

Accompanying was also a joy to me. I accompanied singers and instrumentalists during college years.

Participating in chamber music was a rarer but exhilarating experience, too. And hearing a good string quartet in the intimacy of a small hall was heaven. Solo piano performance left me somewhat cold, part of which was anticipating a paralyzing stage-fright—one which never really happened but which I always feared. Playing *with* people was a different thing, a shared experience, the joy of making music together.

Redeemer Church, Houston, presented some unique challenges in the music arena. The first was to be patient while the old order gave way to the new. From the start I showed up at choir rehearsal just to sing, since that's what I always did. The choir consisted of a quartet of overpowering professional voices and a few volunteers. New to me was the near-torture of enduring the rehearsals. Having been taught by my mother "if you can't say something nice about someone don't say anything at all," I will say no more about the director. Mercifully, before long it became obvious to him that he and the new rector were not reading from the same page regarding matters musical and liturgical. Although his abrupt departure just before Christmas was difficult, it was a relief to tread water for awhile with a well-meaning volunteer organist from the parish. His major shortcoming was playing the pedal parts on a 16' stop on the manuals, creating musical mud. This was to compensate for having no feet—for the organ pedals. Well, I didn't have feet for the organ either, so I could sympathize. Up ahead, much excitement loomed on the horizon.

It happened in stages. First, Graham hired a choir director from a Methodist background, a high school choral director named Tom Lively. Lively, who was certainly livelier than his predecessor, brought with him a young talented high school tenor, plus the boy's father, to reinforce our choir's meager male section. Little did we guess that this young tenor Gary Miles would discover his life vocation in music while in our midst, and spend a good part of his life living, singing, playing the organ, composing, and traveling with the Fisherfolk. In addition to his obvious musical gifts, he had a wicked sense of humor—that came out a bit later.

Somehow we made it through the spring of 1965, when we were presented a remarkable heaven-sent gift: an organist named Kathleen Thomerson who lived in New Orleans but was summering with her parents in Houston. She found out through a musician friend that her old music theory teacher and priest/husband now had a church in the city. Kathleen was looking for a place to practice, so *voilà*. Suddenly we had not just an ordinary organist, for which we would have been grateful, but an extraordinary one. Does God smile? Surely He was smiling on us the day that came about. As usual, the Almighty was accomplishing several things at once. Not only were we getting an accomplished organist for the summer, and she a place to practice regularly: the Lord was also answering a heart-hunger of Kathleen's. She wanted more than anything else to be a *worshipper*, and knew that her professional skills and duties *could* put her at arm's distance from experiencing herself as a worshipper. She had prayed that the Lord would intervene if this ever happened. He was doing it. The fruit of her renewal as a worshipper-with-musical-gifts is apparent in many songs that began to pour forth in her life, beginning with the now—famous hymn, *I Want to Walk as a Child of the Light*.

Things were opening up for my own musical service to the church. For one thing, there were families who had moved into the East End specifically to be part of the renewal that was going on. Their children like our own needed access to things like piano lessons, and these were in short supply in a changing neighborhood. Since there were too many children for me to teach singly, I explored a then-popular class teaching method. It accustomed students to playing in many keys and learning to accompany a simple melody—skills that seemed extremely useful in encouraging music from a community perspective. Several afternoons a week you could find me camped out in the basement choir-room of the church, teaching small classes ranging from four to six. It was fun—a contribution I felt good about making, one consonant with my college degree and training. It was more than that. Now I felt myself to be genuinely a part of the mission we were on. I really *had* received power to step out and do the things the Lord needed and was calling me to do.

One of them was becoming director of the Redeemer Choir, which was growing by leaps and bounds now that folk were beginning to move *into* rather than *out of* this neighborhood. All of them were coming because of our church, and the choir was a place both to serve and to socialize and get to know your neighbors better. I remembered that in the first year, after the departure of the former director, Graham had mentioned to the vestry that I was a professional musician. They had been most hesitant to move forward in my direction, and I can understand why. Having the rector's wife as the choir director could lead to a very sticky situation if things didn't work out well. So I had never been asked—until now.

Now was different, and now was the perfect time. Renewing winds were blowing about the church all over this land and new liturgical texts were evolving. The late sixties proved to be a watershed experience for church composers and I was no exception—except that until now I had not *identified* myself— nor had anyone else—as a church composer. Even now I didn't think that way; there was too much to do, too many services to prepare for, too many intriguing possibilities for arranging music to meet the needs of our group of non-professional but very willing singers. We were on the move and I was swept along in a tide of joy and creativity the likes of which are hard to describe. Music was everywhere; it seemed to be coming up through the *floorboards.*

Another aspect of my musical service was that of being piano accompanist for our evening service on Friday night. Graham had noted that the Sunday school teachers were in dire need of training, of good sound Biblical teaching *themselves*—if they were to educate our children in the faith of their fathers and mothers. His idea was to bring them together *with their families*—for a potluck supper once a week, followed by some basic Bible teaching which he would provide, and a few songs sprinkled in to sweeten the pot. Well, it worked like a charm, and soon more and more people were coming, whether they were teachers or not. There was a hunger out there for the word of God, for learning and growing in the Christian experience. The service took place in Teleph Hall in the basement of the church. I had a love-hate relationship with the old piano there: I loved the fact that we could use the piano in this more informal service; I hated that I had to pick up one out of every four keys before it would sound again—due to high humidity in the basement. No organist pulling multiple stops has ever been kept busier than I was pulling stuck keys on the Teleph Hall piano.

We might have remained "stuck" in the basement forever except for a flood God sent our way. I'm *sure* God did it. Until now no one had even *considered* the possibility of having this sort of service in the main nave of the church. We would feel swallowed up in all that space, surely. But when the flooding happened, it was like God saying, "Friends, come up higher." We were transported from that dark, damp basement into the light once again. No one was happier about it than I, for now I could play a *real* piano with keys that didn't stick.

It was a good thing that I had been teaching the children how to play in many different keys, because now I was constantly faced with that challenge myself. It would happen this way: Friday night soon morphed into a prayer and praise service drawing people from all over the greater Houston area. There were Baptists, there were Roman Catholics, some of them nuns, there were folk from every conceivable Christian background, and there were some of our un-churched neighbors as well, drawn there out of curiosity if nothing else. We sang hymns and songs from a wide spectrum, many Scripture-based choruses as well as new songs from people in the congregation. There were also times of "waiting on the Spirit"—times when anyone could offer a prayer, or a word of encouragement, or a word of prophecy, or . . . yes, a song. These songs would be started by one of the flock, in a key of their own choosing, and mine would be the task of accompanying whatever it was so that others could join in. Thanks to the gift of a good sense of relative pitch, I could spot most of the keys without a problem. Sometimes I would have to play a key on the piano *softly* to ascertain which was the nearest key to what was being sung, since the human voice is not a *well-tempered clavier.*

My favorite memories are the times when Bill Farra, functioning as song leader, would start a song in his favorite key, F# Major. That's the key with only *six sharps. Come on, Bill; give me a break*, I used to think. But then, I just got used to playing everything he threw my way with my fingers dancing around those black keys. *Now . . .* it's just plain funny. The real magic in these times was very close to what jazzers experience with their improvisations: you never knew where it all would lead, but in our case we were trusting God's spirit to be in the mix—and also trusting our own humanity enough to lead out a song if we were so moved. There was a wonderful freedom in this.

The Redeemer Choir proved an invaluable training-ground for people on a journey spiritually. Here there were no primadonnas, although we had lots of very talented folk as choir members. Many of them sang in the *Way In Coffeehouse*, one of the early outreach ministries of the parish. But here the Spirit was blending many voices into *one* voice, as in II Chronicles 5. And this was really about the intentional blending of lives together, the voices serving as an outward sign of an inward work that was happening in us all. Graham was always a member of the choir. He saw the symbolic value of this blending of voices and submitted himself—and *his* voice—to the process. This was one of the ways—as I look back on it—he was modeling what it means for the ordained minister to "mix" it with the laity. He simply became one of them in the choir. And he was a good choir member. He had a *krummhorn* bass voice, a reedy bass, and he knew how to blend with other more string-like voices.

We had great solo-type voices too. There was the aforementioned tenor Gary Miles. There was Mikel Kennedy, folk-singer *extraordinaire*. The extraordinary thing was by no means his gravelly voice—not really a pretty voice—but his charism and vocal style. There was Jodi Page, Mike's female counterpart, a gifted vocal stylist who made you think you were back in the hills of West Virginia. And then there was Mimi Armstrong with her classically trained, beautiful soprano voice. We had it all. These were the early days. Later on there was Diane Davis, another soprano with a hauntingly beautiful voice. All of these talented folk sang in the choir, and sitting beside any one of them might be an ordinary member who could not read music and was just learning to match tones. So, from the very start the idea of helping your neighbor was a given in the Redeemer Choir. That's what it was all about. We were not a choral society, or a guild. We were learning how to *be* a community and singing together was one of the ways we learned.

Then there was the coffeehouse—the place where all these young artists *did* get to be soloists and share their God-given talent, combined with their own personal testimony about how the Holy Spirit had brought them here, or was moving in their lives. Youth groups from churches all over the county and beyond began to flock to the *Way In* coffeehouse on Friday and Saturday evenings. This was a happening place. Our intention had been to establish a ministry near Allen's Landing, a hippie hangout in the city, and minister to the "hippies." Much preparation had gone on—including sending a team of our young lay ministers to New York to train in street ministry. The Lord had the final say, and this turned out to be primarily a ministry to youth from churches all over Harris County and as far afield as Huntsville. Sometimes when we set out to serve, it's the setting out that really counts, and the Lord adjusts the compass once we're underway. At least, that's how I figure it.

Even I, at the tender age of forty, suited up and sang at the *Way In* coffeehouse on occasion; there were no fixed age restrictions. I remember wearing one of those pant-dresses—or was it a pajama-suit? Anyway, it was popular at the time, full-skirted and you stepped into it. It was a bright silky flowered thing, and made me feel very young indeed. I have always thought that it's the close association with people younger than myself that has kept me *thinking young*—even though I may not look the part.

There were many *moments musicale* on the journey, things that stand out in memory's treasure-trove as priceless times. One was towards the close of a Friday night service when someone started singing the familiar *Eight-fold Alleluia*, and pretty soon you could hear full four-part harmony emanating from the entire congregation. Then my voice just "lifted off" in a descant none of us knew or had heard before. We were singing with the angels, adoring our Lord and Savior Jesus Christ. For that space of time and in that moment we were in the heavenlies *already*. That was the night I discovered the full meaning of *ecstasy* in worship. We had been lifted out of our ordinariness into the palpable presence of God. This was not the only time such a thing happened there, but it stands out because of my own particular involvement.

Many *moments musicale* related directly to people at Redeemer Church. One was Jeff Schiffmayer, our new Associate Rector who had come straight off the mission field in Malawi. Jeff used to reminisce with great nostalgia about the singing of the African Christians. He missed particularly the way men's and women's voices sang back and forth antiphonally; he had come to appreciate the beauty of these contrasting high and low voices. His comments planted a seed in my soul, a longing that our singing could emulate that quality Jeff was describing. *Glory to God*—from the *King of Glory* setting for Eucharist was my musical response. It was in no way a conscious response to Jeff's longings; it was the Spirit's response, and I was the musical emissary. Sure enough, it had a section where men's and women's voices sang in canon, a real liturgical duet. It should be sub-titled "Jeff's Song" because it was, and remains so to me. He inspired it.

Another relational happening involved the *Keyhole* group who sang at the *Way In* coffeehouse. One spring, as we headed into the Easter season, I was smitten by the *Song of Moses* text from Exodus 15. Not surprisingly, as the music took shape in my head—which is to say in my ears—it had a distinct Hebraic flavor. We had been exploring and enjoying folk dances, especially the Israeli circle dances, as corporate expressions of joy. So from the first this felt like one of those; that was not surprising. What surprised me was that the verses I began to "hear" in my head were being sung by Ed Baggett, one of the *Keyhole* group. This was thrilling to me, because it confirmed what was already in my heart: I was writing music for *people*—for people I knew, for people with whom I worked, lived, for people I loved. This was a special *moment musicale.*

Other such moments happened with my own children. There was nine-year-old Jane who heard the gentle falling rain outside her window as the tears of Jesus who was praying for us in heaven. That was a poignant moment, because at the time two of Graham's sisters were visiting us and I could sense a reconciling work of the Spirit going on in this family which had at one time been so torn apart over religion. Graham's mother, who had dutifully rejected her son in obedience to Rome, had later been told by her post-Vatican II priest that she should seek out her son and forgive him. She *did* reach out to Graham and was planning to visit us when she passed away in 1968. So . . . the tears of Jesus? Yes. I wrote the *Rain Song* that very afternoon.

There was one *Handelian* experience. Inspired by new liturgical texts in the Episcopal Church's book of trial liturgies, I sat down at the piano and composed the *Melchizedek Mass* on one Sunday afternoon in 1970. I still remember the place I was sitting, the particular piano, how the room *felt*, the whole thing. It was a musical mission of some sort, though I didn't fully comprehend what it was: It was to synthesize the traditional music of the church with a new wave of folk-oriented music which was pulsing through us as well. Both had to fit somehow into our Sunday liturgy. It was not o.k. for the coffee-house music and the Sunday music to remain separate. Weren't we *all* a vital part of the church? Then, if that were the case, the music of *all* must find expression in this weekly liturgy where we brought *everything* and *everyone* together. We put it all "in the bread" as our friend Benedict Reid was fond of saying. So that's what this new setting for Eucharist was all about. It combined organ, four-part choral parts and guitar. Here was the synthesis I was looking for. What better name for this setting than the name of Melchizedek, symbol of the eternal priesthood of Christ? As for Handel, he spent much more than a Sunday afternoon writing *Messiah*, but after my experience on that particular afternoon I understood what had gripped him and kept him on task until the task was done.

There were times when I was called to do something I felt ill-equipped to do. One was in the late sixties when we were living in the MacGregor house, with eleven children in the household. Each Redeemer household had a special focus and ours was a ministry to children; we had quite a headstart with six of our own to 'sweeten the pot.' At the church we were launching a week-night gathering of families—a time to share a potluck supper, some singing and fellowship, and to feature a Bible story enacted by one of the participating families. Guess who got to go first? It's a no-brainer: the rector's family. We were assigned—which is to say, Graham volunteered us for—the story of Rebecca. We had little preparation time: maybe one day, two at the most. As I carried the name "Rebecca" with me on supermarket runs, it struck me as a very musical name. A song, methinks: a song with a simple, singable refrain; I'll make up some verses that tell the story, and the children can act it out. So that's what we did. Our *only* run through with children was sandwiched in between the time school let out that afternoon and 5:30 when we were due at the church. To say it was not a polished performance is an understatement; it was barely together, and extremely rough-hewn. That was the whole point, as it turned out—to do something others would not be afraid to follow when it was *their* turn. On this occasion and many others, I have been comforted by the words of G.K. Chesterton who famously said, "Whatever is worth doing, is worth doing *badly*"

The good news is: other families did step up to the plate and act out stories on successive nights. So—it worked.

The summer of 1969 held a special surprise for us all. By this time the Redeemer Choir had weathered some fairly challenging anthems ranging from Gibbons to Vaughan Williams and beyond. Summer is typically *not* the time to do anything fancy—that is, if your church is an assemblage of middle-class families all of whom go on vacations during the summer months. Ours was not. We had bought into a way of living that held us accountable for others' summers, not just our own. There were many in our households who did *not* have summer holidays, or if they did, lacked the financial resources to do much more than drive to Galveston for a day at the beach. Together we needed to create some beauty, some challenges, some great moments right where we were. So, we decided on an August performance of the Faure *Requiem*. Certainly it met some of those criteria. But it also sent a few shock-waves around Houston's musically elite circles—that the likes of *us* would be performing the likes of *that* in the East End . . . and in *August*. It would also bring into our midst— as a "keeper"—one of the most conspicuous musical talents around: that of George Mims. He had been visiting services and definitely seemed drawn to the place and our mission. Knowing his background as an organist/director, and finding myself close to overloaded at the prospect of getting all this together in time, I asked George to direct the choir for the performance. He had far more directing experience than I. He agreed, and a bond was created that bore fruit for years to come.

> *Hallelujah! Praise the Name of the Lord;*
> *give praise, you servants of the Lord,*
> *You who stand in the house of the Lord,*
> *in the courts of the house of our God.*
> *Psalm 135: 1-2*

Fourteen
A Journey Of The Heart

The Church with Psalms must shout,
no door can keep them out;
but above all, the heart must bear the longest part.
George Herbert (1593-1633)

As my musical journey had led me into new territories, another adventure was in process. It was a journey of the heart, without which the musical journey would have become a tinkling cymbal. The heart journey was all about the adventures of learning to love.

My heart-journey, like my musical one, had deep roots in childhood. As a teenager I was independent and oftimes contentious, frequently put on a pedestal and considered aloof. My heart was well defended. It's hard to feel very deeply when you have a well-defended heart; your energies are spent largely in protecting yourself from being hurt. I was good at this. Some of these defense mechanisms had served me well when I stepped out into the wide world on my own, fresh out of college. I can still hear the deafening silence on the other end of the line when I told my parents about accepting a job more than a thousand miles away in a place where I knew no one. They were shocked, as most parents of that era would have been when a *daughter* chose such a path. They needn't have worried too much, because I was well defended.

When had my armor begun to crack? When had my heart begun to feel? When had I allowed myself to be hurt? Only by degrees and in stages. Because I married young—twenty-two seems *very* young these days—my relationship to Graham was center-stage in this process. As I have already indicated, he was different than the southern boys I had known and dated. He never scurried around the car to open the door for me when we went places together. *What a shock.* I can remember just sitting there in full anticipation of this chivalrous behavior. It never happened—oh, maybe he came around once to humor me and get me out of the car; but he let me know that it was not something he could be expected to remember on a regular basis. Then there were the manifold times I asked him to do something by saying, "Wouldn't you like to . . . . ?" He would look at me thoughtfully, then say, "No." He was not angry; he was just answering the question. If I had been nearly as honest I might have framed the question differently: "*Shouldn't* you like to . . . ?" Because it was assumed in my southern book of unwritten etiquette that of course he would like to do *whatever* pleased me. My glass house was already getting a few chinks in it.

That was good, if disconcerting: good to be shaken loose from thinking the whole world was southern, that every utterance needed mixing with magnolia juice before serving, that plain talk needed sugar-coating. I learned all of that in spades with Graham, who was himself a highly cultured, intelligent person; he just wasn't *southern*—unless southern Canada counts. Our first year of marriage saw many of these international communications crises, and I allowed him to trample on some of my *souther-en-ness*. I am not sure what *he* learned, other than the fact that when you marry a southerner there are a heck of a lot of unspoken expectations that you are likely to bump into just any time. Marrying someone from a different corner of the world does have advantages, like seeing ourselves as others see us. Perhaps it helps us be more flexible and tolerant. But easy it is not.

Having children was for me another course in the *learning to love* curriculum. I have known dedicated teachers who loved children as much as their own parents—sometimes more, so pro-creation has no guarantee of producing loving behavior. When I read about parents' physical abuse of children I often think, "There, but for the grace of God, go I," recalling my own times of frustration and insecurity as a young mother. Once in February when baby Mary was less than two months old and I was struggling through feeding problems with her, a cold spell hit the Florida Keys. The jalousied windows of the bedroom simply would not close tight enough to keep out the frigid winds that were blowing outside. Graham was at sea; my mother Bey and I were grasping at straws to keep the baby warm. We put a hot water bottle at the bottom of her small crib to warm the covers a bit. Then she got too warm and caught a cold. One day, feeling so frightened and incompetent and so concerned for this tiny six-pound morsel of humanity, I picked her up while in this agitated state. Now I can understand how seemingly rational adults end up shaking babies. I came perilously close. All of a sudden this little creature looked up at me from her receiving blanket with the most incredulous expression on her tiny face. She seemed to say to me without any words,

"What are you *doing?*" I wept. Babies, tiny tots, growing children and teenagers—all have much to teach us about what love is, and isn't.

The biggest challenges in learning to love happened as we expanded our household in the sixties and began to relate to other adults as part of *us*. Our friend Virginia taught me that the word "us' has an interesting metamorphosis as we grow up. Initially it means our family of origin, then when we leave home and marry it means husband and wife, then when we have kids it means father and mother and however many kids there are. All of this derives from a nuclear family pattern of thinking. What we were discovering in Houston was more like the extended family pattern of my grandparents' time, more like a clan or tribe—though we did not have time to sit and rock and ruminate over the sociology of it all. It was a *God-thing* that was going on.

The initial expansion of our rectory household to include three young adults alongside ourselves and our six children was an easy transition compared with moving to the North Main house where the coffeehouse ministry began. My heavens, now we are twenty! How did we get *here?* What does *us* mean now? I can recall crying out to the Lord, *"How can I love this many people at once?"* Some place deep inside the still small voice said to me, "Just love one person at a time." That was the balm of Gilead on my troubled soul. Yes, I thought, I can tackle that: just loving one person at a time. That is something I just may be able to handle.

Just. It worked most of the time, but I had a continuing struggle in my soul with Bill Farra. You may wonder why I always referred to him by his first *and* last names, so let me assure you that even his wife Mimi did the same during that period. It started when he came to live in the rectory household where there was already a Bill— our oldest son. So he became universally known by both names, which his wonderful parents, Maris and Margaret, must have found slightly peculiar.

Bill Farra had come to us as a broken-hearted young widower. He stayed to become a man of deep spirituality and wisdom and infinite usefulness in God's kingdom. This was a process and Graham was his mentor; they spent much time together. As part of Bill's growth in ministry, Graham would include him in certain counseling sessions, primarily as a listener and learner and intercessor. According to how needy I was feeling at the moment, Graham seemed to me to be spending inordinate amounts of time with Bill and not enough with me. That may well have been the case; but also, my own subterranean homophobic fears were stewing away deep inside: defending my turf and lashing out were the only ways I knew to express them. The *acting out* happened infrequently and seldom in front of others in the household.

After one particular night, when around eleven pm I pounded on a window in Graham's office, separated from the rectory by only a carport, pounded on that window because I knew Graham and Bill were there, pounded on that window until I broke it with my bare hands: after that particular night they knew. So did Dr. Bob who sewed up the hand that went through the window. My rage was, if not common knowledge, at least *felt* by others. How I wish I could have rewritten that chapter, or that I had had more resources to bring to bear on the situation, or that *they* had. The saving grace at the rectory was that we did have other adults in the household, so we were able to live in peace and harmony most of the time. The real battle was going on inside of *me*.

By the time we moved to North Main house, with twenty people, Bill's leadership amongst the young adults was well established, and he was worth his weight in gold. There were humorous moments, as when Bill was explaining to the Redeemer Friday-night congregation, a packed house, just when and how our household was moving from the nice rectory next-door to a derelict house in north Houston. Many were puzzled about the rector and his family with small children taking off for a crime-ridden part of the city. Bill assured them that some cosmetic treatments were happening to make the old house more livable, and that the school-aged children would be ferried in to school so there would be no mid-year disruption of their education.

"Unfortunately," he told them, we will not be able to take along our pet dachshund *Katie* because"—here he paused to find a simple way to tell them there was no fenced yard for Katie—"because the place really isn't *fit* for a dog." His words hung in the air for a moment before the entire congregation was convulsed in laughter.

One night I was sitting near Bill on the staircase of the North Main house. The living room was full of household members, all gathered to decide on a name for the new coffeehouse. We were located just a block away from a railroad overpass, with North Main Street running below. As cars emerged from the tunnel and the road began to ascend, ours was the house at the top of the hill. It was like coming out of darkness into light. An idea struck me.

"We could call it *The Way Out*," I said. Everyone pondered that for a minute, then Bill said,

"How about *The Way In?*" And a coffeehouse ministry was born.

Once the coffeehouse ministry was up and running, the rector's household moved from our mission outpost back to a rectory nearer the church, purchased with our extended household in mind. A Colonial-style house on North MacGregor Drive, it was a gracious and lovely home framed by big oak trees laced with Spanish moss. Braes Bayou ran directly in front of it. Redeemer Church had been able to purchase it for a song because the area was beginning to feel the effects of *white flight*, an exodus to the suburbs due to an enlarging black population to the east. Real estate prices had fallen and we were the definite beneficiaries. Guess what? Before long, and once again, we had close to twenty people in *this* house as well. Maybe it was just eighteen.

Since households assumed particular roles and identities, ours had an inevitable ministry to children, as we had eleven in our midst. Six were ours, four belonged to Virginia, our friend from Austin days who had surfaced again after a painful divorce and a move to Houston. The other, a teenage girl, was the daughter of a divorcee who had come to Redeemer for healing ministry and had stayed.

Having a mother with four children as part of the fabric of the household was a new experience—read my lips *challenge*—for me. Here was yet another lesson in the learning to love syllabus. Here was an intelligent and gifted woman, a social worker by profession, who had run her own household for years, and because of the end of a marriage, had found herself drawn in our direction. Not only that: she had brought furniture with her! It wasn't just *any* furniture: it was her grandmother's antique dining table and rickety chairs. Now the stage was set for the dilemma my father had faced back in the Great Depression when he and a friend had contemplated buying a house together: they had reckoned that two women simply could not share a kitchen together, and that was that. In our case, the issue was the dining-room. *Whose dining room furniture goes into the dining room?*

The answer was so simple as to be elusive at first. Because the household was large we actually needed both tables, and ours, being the smaller, fit handily in the front hallway. Virginia's fit beautifully in the dining room as the primary table. That was our first, though certainly not our last, crisis in sharing family values and "stuff." It was also very much part of learning to love, which a lot of the time is really learning to sift through what's important and separate it from what's *less* important. The funny part is that now—forty plus years later—my children and I frequently put our feet under that same dining room table and sit in those same rickety chairs, which now beautify Virginia's home in Austin, Texas.

Community living brought to the fore mutual accountability for children—by definition the dependent members. For us, parents' role with their own children was paramount. There were times however, when adults other than parents needed to assume responsibility for one or more of the children over a space of time. Not all adults have the same style or grace or effectiveness in this role. There were lessons of forbearance to be learned here: Once I came home to discover that the *nanny* for the afternoon, a nice young woman, had disciplined four-year-old David for saying a bad word by washing his mouth out with soap. This was not a technique I would have chosen, and in fact it sounded Dickensian to me—but?? I had left her in charge, and it was just one of those things. David still loves to tell about it; he doesn't appear to have been terminally damaged. But make no mistake: this was another of those lessons about loving. Loving includes forbearance. We had embraced into our lives a large number of people bearing many and different gifts, and all of them were, like ourselves, imperfect.

Graham used to say, "Think of the person in your circle of friends and family whom you love *least*. This is an accurate measure of how much you love Jesus Christ." *Say it isn't so.*

There are "testers' sent into every life, and at every stage of life, it seems. Too often I have related to such folk as necessary evils: people that somehow have to be endured. But, seen in this light it is not ok for me just to tolerate them; I must actually learn to *love them*. Oh, help. No wonder St. Paul exhorted Christians to "work out their salvation with fear and trembling." The demands of love are great, if we are talking about the love of God as seen in the life, passion, death and resurrection of Jesus Christ. This *is* our life work—*learning to love*.

There was a touching moment with my 104-year-old mother the day before she died, when she asked my forgiveness for something. We had found it necessary to put her in respite care over the Christmas holidays. For some time she had been having brief spells of dementia, probably linked to an earlier stroke. Now she imagined me to be the *enemy*, since I was the one who had made the decision. But the Spirit of the Lord and of the deep places of her life showed her that she was being harsh in her judgment of me. One of her final acts at the end of a loving life was this: to reach out and ask forgiveness for judging me harshly. She simply said, several times over and over, "I've been wrong; I've been wrong." Would I have had that kind of grace in a moment of such extremity? Could I turn, and ask forgiveness? I hope so. She was still learning to love—right to the end of her remarkable life.

> *Your love, O Lord, for ever will I sing;*
> *from age to age my mouth will proclaim your faithfulness.*
>
> *For I am persuaded that your love is established for ever;*
> *you have set your faithfulness firmly in the heavens.*
>
> Psalm 89: 1—2

Fifteen
Across The Waters

What's love got to do with it? Everything. What about geography? Geography's got a lot to do with it, too. The places I have lived have left a deep impact on my life. Living and visiting are fundamentally different. When you ride a tour-bus, you generally know where you're going to get off. But when you are living somewhere it's not so easy. In a certain sense you *become* a part of the life around you, involved in the culture around you, and attached to the people around you. Graham had a different view of all this: he used to say that anywhere you dwelled longer than twenty-four hours you needed to consider permanent. It was with this in mind that he taught our children, when we went camping in the summer, always to leave the campsite better than we found it. Let your footprint be a positive one, in other words. It wasn't so much how long you spent somewhere; it was *how* you spent the time you had been given that mattered. And somewhere in this process, we learned about stewardship, about taking care of the *things* around us as well as caring for the *people* around us. Life's boundaries extended somehow.

How did we come to go across the waters to live? For me, it was a song that sent us across the waters in 1972. I didn't recognize it for what it was at the time: a prophetic summons to a life of discipleship. Even now I am probably the only person alive who thinks of it that way. But for me that's what it is. A simple hymn-text by William Percy riveted my attention in 1971.

There was a musical setting of it in the Episcopal Hymnal 1940 which I had enjoyed singing. There was something about those words that wouldn't leave me alone:

> *They cast their nets in Galilee, just off the hills of brown;*
> *Such happy, simple fisherfolk before the Lord came down.*
>
> *Contented, peaceful fishermen, before they ever knew*
> *The peace of God that filled their hearts brimful, and broke them, too.*
>
> *Young John, who trimmed the flapping sail, homeless in Patmos died. Peter, who hauled the teeming net, head-down was crucified.*
>
> *The peace of God, it is no peace, but strife closed in the sod, Yet let us pray for but one thing: the marvelous peace of God.*
>
> Wm. Alexander Percy (1885-1942)[3]

I found myself reading and re-reading these words. Then I began to hear lapping waves somewhere in my head—how I imagined the gentle waves on the Sea of Galilee might sound. Then, with the gentle lapping waves, a tune emerged through the mist of my mind. The tune seemed to fit the ballad quality of the words, which tell a simple story—a story with a poignant ending. Embedded in the text is the word *fisherfolk,* though I took no particular note of it at the time. It turned out to be a prophetic word for us.

In 1970 CBS Religious News had contacted Church of the Redeemer, wanting to do a half-hour documentary film about the remarkable growth and renewal going on there. In the process they found so much material that they decided to make it an hour-long show. It was an exciting time for the parish, a little

---

[3] Words Copyright, Edward B. Marks Music Corp.

unnerving to be honest. None of us had had film experience or seemed like "naturals" in front of a camera. However, Mimi Armstrong had trained as an operatic soprano and had stage presence galore, and now that she had added folk guitar to her bag of tricks CBS took quick note of her and she became the star of the show. That was tantamount to "putting our best foot forward." Graham was also very much at ease in front of a camera and extemporizing was his forte. None of us could have guessed what an impact this film would have, and in a certain sense you could say it was the CBS documentary *Following the Spirit* that sent us across the waters.

Away over in England, Cuthbert Bardsley, the Anglican bishop of Coventry, viewed the film in May 1971. Graham had been asked to speak to the clergy of his diocese. Bill Farra was there with him, and they decided to show the film which CBS had first aired on television on Pentecost 1971. The bishop's sister also saw it and her response was:

"Look, Cuthbert. It's just like—*during the war!*"

By this she meant a *good* thing. The commonality of the life she saw portrayed, the mutual concerns acted out before her eyes spoke to her of a time she had known when people all over Britain moved out beyond selfish interests, beyond class boundaries, to embrace and help one another. That time was World War II.

Another fruit of this clergy meeting was an invitation from a local Coventry priest who needed help in his parish and inquired whether Bill Farra could come over and help *him*—as he had helped a priest in New Zealand earlier. Graham's quick response to this had been, "Sure—if he can bring his household with him." Clearly, by this time the lay ministers who had been through Redeemer Church's untitled school of Christian formation were in demand. Somehow, out of all of this—an interested bishop, and a priest needing help in his parish—came an invitation for us to come spend extended time in the Coventry Diocese.

Back home in Houston the new plan threw things into high gear. Getting a household of sixteen ready for such a venture was challenging. In the end, we were all up for it and excited about the opportunity to live overseas. Virginia was magnificent at preparing the children for the adventure. We checked out library books about customs, foods, colloquial sayings in the United Kingdom, all designed to rev-up the kids and get them excited. It did. There were personal struggles, of course, and as usual struggling seemed to be one of my strong suits. Change has always been hard for me, and living in an extended family setting didn't ease the struggle. Well, it probably *did*—otherwise I might have fallen by the wayside somewhere.

The journey across the waters was memorable in capital letters. We went by land and by air and by sea, quite literally. First, we had to deal with ministry commitments already on the books for August, involving Graham and Bill primarily. Then we had to deal with good-byes to family members in the Carolinas. We had a sense of urgency about getting to England in time for the children to enroll at the beginning of the school year. So our strategy was "divide and conquer." Half of us took the high road through Tennessee and the Carolinas, half took the low road along the Gulf coast, rendezvousing in Fort Lauderdale, Florida to catch our Air Bahamas flight to Luxembourg. The strategy went smoothly, accompanied by bumps and lurches of grief-pangs which all were experiencing, to be sure, though we were far too busy keeping up with children and luggage to give our grieving much thought.

Keeping up with the luggage was the easier part. We had forty-eight pieces between us, each person having been allotted one suitcase for clothing plus a box for books and personal stuff; then there were musical instruments as well. *Each* of the forty-eight pieces had a big circle of contact paper stuck onto it, bright yellow and orange and flowered all-over contact paper—the sort of thing used to line shelves. Credit or blame *me* for the luggage décor. Then, with a black marking pen we numbered each piece #1 through #48, and there you had it. There was no way under heaven that you could miss one of our pieces of luggage. The garish, crude marking system worked like a charm. Some months later Bill Farra and I attended a guitar workshop at Coventry Cathedral. As we climbed the steps to go in, Bill looked down at our guitar cases, clearly marked # 18 and # 42. He laughed, "They are going to think we're part of a *really big* outfit."

Keeping up with kids was not quite so straightforward. We devised a buddy system where each child had an adult *buddy*—bless their little hearts. *Both* needed blessing. The system was handy for transitioning moments from vehicle to air terminal, concourse to concourse, check-in to boarding gate, train to train with only minutes to spare, ferry to taxi-cab to overnight accommodation. We had it all to do and there were a thousand places you could have lost a child along the way. None were lost, praise God. After a brief taxi-tour of Kingston, Jamaica which made me nostalgic for the fifties' songs of Harry Belafonte, we caught our overnight flight to Europe—*the night that never was.* Then we trained to Amsterdam where we spent the next night and ate enormous duck-eggs for breakfast.

Then on to the English Channel and a ferry trip across to Harwich on the east coast of England. By the time we reached Liverpool Station in London twilight was setting in. A large coach had been hired to drive us across the city to our hosts' home. Had the coach drivers been briefed about providing a scenic tour? While I can't say for sure, I do know their main job was to take us to the Harper's where we were to bed down for the night. On route we saw Trafalgar Square, Buckingham Palace, Big Ben, and much more. Yes, this was the place, we thought. *This is London.*

Whenever I remember our brief touch-down visit with Michael and Jeanne Harper, St. Paul's words come to mind about ministering "in season and out of season." Their house was being re-wired, and some of the floorboards had been taken up to facilitate this. Also, there was no electricity, so we had candlelight processions to our bedrooms. There a bed was waiting for each of us, a bed with fresh linens, covers pulled back ready to receive weary travelers, *and*—wonder of British wonders—a *hottie,* or hot-water bottle, warming the bottom of each bed. Having spent the night in many homes since, I have never felt more genuinely welcomed and warmly received. I have always translated St. Paul's words into my own life by thinking of "in season" as something convenient, and "out of season" as something quite inconvenient. This was by definition *inconvenient* for the Harpers, but you would never have guessed it by the quality of hospitality they offered us.

It was in many ways a story-book welcome to England—full of surprises like duck eggs for breakfast, a twilight tour of London and exotic candlelight processions to bed. We were well launched into our "English period." Now we made our way to Coventry where our first English dwelling-place awaited us.

Here the atmosphere was more like . . . down-to-earth with a thud. Not that anything went wrong exactly.

The whole story came out much later. It seems that the details of our accommodation had been left in the hands of the local priest in whose parish we would be living. That entailed a good deal of trans-Atlantic communication between himself and Graham. But here was the stinger: shortly before our departure from Houston Graham had been notified that the house we had expected to live in would not be available after all and that we needed to wait until another could be secured. Graham's response had been,

"It's too late for us to change plans now. We are on our way. Do your best to find a place, and I'll be praying."

He never said a peep to any of us about it; he took the whole weight of it on himself. He *believed* God had told us to go, as surely as old Abraham had believed when he set out from Ur of the Chaldees to Haran. Therefore he trusted that God would provide a place for us. God did. But how often I have looked back with compassion on this man, this brave husband of mine who took such a giant step of faith and never flinched. He knew the bald truth of the situation would have left many of us feeling vulnerable in the extreme. For sure he knew that about me. So he just bowed the knees of his heart before the Lord on our behalf. Thank you, Graham.

Eighteen Milner Crescent—an address I will never forget. Here we are in Coventry in our semi-detached—read my lips: *too small*—house. We have finally arrived at our new home-away-from-home. Sure enough, we *do* have a roof over our heads. And none of us knew how close we had come to *not* having one. This was a good place to put our American capacity for ingenuity and problem-solving to work: converting the garage into a dining room—the only way to seat all of us at one table. This worked fine except for anxious moments when a vehicle wheeled into the driveway, slamming on its brakes within inches of the person seated at the head of the table. The startled look on that person's face was indescribable. Multiple bunk-beds were put up in the bedrooms. We lined the narrow front hallway with coat-hooks where we could hang our coats, rendering it impossible to walk down the hall in normal fashion—we shuffled down sideways to avoid knocking off the coats. The English obviously did not believe in closets as we had known them in America; not only was there no coat closet, there were no closets, *period.* Nor was there room for one of those space-guzzling wardrobes the English regard so fondly; we lived out of our suitcases mostly. We did have coat-hooks in a back utility room where each of us could hang one outfit apiece. It was a bit like camping out, only you were inside and someone had forgotten the marshmallows for roasting.

Our living-room, known to the English as a *lounge,* was small but several people could sit and chat there. Virginia and I wanted it to be a pleasant room for all, so we went into the City Centre of Coventry to look for something in the way of décor to enhance our lounge. In a thrift shop we found it—a large painting of sheep grazing in a hazy sort of pasture, with dim haystacks and a shepherd somewhere in the background. The wooden frame was substantial, and nicely finished. We agreed this was a good choice for our bare lounge wall. So we bought it for seventy-five pence, something in the neighborhood of a dollar-and-a-half American money. We were pleased with our bargain "find," never dreaming we had bought a needed icon.

As soon as it was hung and I sat down to look at it, my eye also fell on the old folks' home across the street, clearly visible through the window. It occurred to me that it was just the size home we needed, and I told the Lord so, though I did stop short of coveting *that very* house. I was sure the Lord got the idea. As I gazed at our new sheep picture, some verses from the tenth chapter of John's Gospel came to my remembrance: *He calls his own sheep by name and leads them out . . . He goes ahead of them, and the sheep follow him because they know his voice.* How appropriate. For here we certainly were, at our Lord's own heeding, here we were, the sheep of his pasture, and He had led us a long, long way out from our grazing grounds in Houston. Here we were. What did the Lord have in mind, now that we were here?

Few of us had a clue. It would have to be revealed. So, in the meantime, I would take my morning cup of tea into the lounge, where I could gaze at our picture *and* also across the road at the old folks' home. It became my daily place of prayer: the sheep picture was my icon, leading me into a sense of God's guiding presence with us now; and the old folks' home was my reminder to the Lord that we really *did* need a bigger spot to lay our heads.

Heigh-ho, heigh-ho, it's off to school we go. David at age 4 ½ was in infant school, but you would never have known it judging from the length of the school-day, which ran from *8 a.m. to 4 p m.*—the same as the older kids' day. "Why . . ." he asked plaintively after the first week, "why . . . in England . . . do the children go to school *so much?*"

Why, indeed. The "middle-aged" kids were in junior school and seemed to adapt well—except that Jane came home crying every day for the first couple of weeks since she couldn't understand a word her teacher was saying. That was due to her *Brummie* accent, a Birmingham working-class brogue which was thick and bore little resemblance to the *Kings' English* on B.B.C. The older children were enrolled in a comprehensive school, which sought primarily to prepare students for learning a trade. In Potters Green, our working-class neighborhood, this was a good match for most of the kids, even if not ideal for ours. Still, ours worked hard to fit in and *not sound American.* As early teenagers, this was a priority for them.

Back in Houston after-school hours had been spent enjoying the great out-of-doors, often in our tremendous back yard, ideal for ball games and such. The children had several hours to unwind after sitting at school-desks all day. But here in Coventry dusk was approaching by the time they came home from school. Heaven help us. Suddenly, confined to this small house, we were running an after-school program to preserve everyone's sanity. *Bring on the music.* Most of the children were learning at least one musical instrument, so practicing became a big part of the after-school drill. I made a cassette tape for Bey while roaming about the house with the "Record" button on, so she could hear for herself the sounds of our junior conservatory—violin, clarinet, recorders, and a couple of guitars—none of them playing on the same page, or even the same piece. This was our afternoon cacophony. Thank God for music.

Once, before we had learned all we needed to know about English gardens behind semi-detached houses—they are small and likely to be full of rose bushes—the children began a game of hide-and-seek in our garden. Martha found herself impaled on a large, healthy rose-bush with fifty thorns embedded beneath her skin. *Ouch.* As the days grew a little longer in the springtime, there were certain afternoons when the children were lured outside by the waning sunshine. The tiny back garden sloped down to a six-foot wooden fence separating us from fields beyond. There was no gate until one afternoon when the kids were taking turns riding a wagon down the slope. On one rapid descent they couldn't—or didn't—stop, and crashed through the fence. Oh, dear; or rather—*Hallelujah.* No one was hurt and only the fence was damaged. From that moment on, the children gained entry to the large field through a gate they themselves had created. For my part, I never said a word to the landlord. Clearly it was divine intervention; God had said "gate" and there was one. We were thankful.

This is my Story This is my Song

Daily adventures like these kept us on our toes and learning new things in a land that was foreign in many ways, though unified by the language we all spoke. We spoke it differently in different places, as Jane had discovered at school. Sometimes we struggled to understand what was being *said,* and sometimes what was *mean*t by the words. We were jollying the children along with their culture shock; but all the while my life felt stark. At least the kids had schools to attend—something structural and expected in their lives. I had nothing—nothing of the ministry activities that had so thoroughly engaged me in Houston, nothing of the joy of music-making with the Redeemer choir. I felt depressed, more than at any time in my life. *But* I had the people I loved—and they proved to be invaluable, *life-saving,* if you will. The thing was: the person I had pledged to honor 'til death us do part was seldom there. This whole Coventry move had come up *after* many ministry commitments had been made by Graham. So he left for substantial hunks of time, going back to the States to fulfill those engagements. I felt abandoned. There was a real and very deep pain in my soul, an agony which penetrated my very bones and marrow. If I had had anywhere to run away to, I would have—that's how desperate I felt. But we had left all those places and possibilities behind. I was stuck.

My close relationship to Virginia and to Bill Farra saved me from jumping ship. Virginia listened to me pour out my heart's cry; and Bill was like a nail in a sure place—he was just always *there*. One evening just before dusk several of us—though not the two of them—took a walk around the neighborhood. I needed oxygen, just to breathe outside air. I needed space. As we walked my awareness grew: that I needed God in this situation more than I had ever needed Him before. *How can I keep going—here in this faraway place, where so little is familiar, and I have no real function?*

"No real function?" the Lord seemed to ask me. "What about your children you have brought with you to this place?"

Suddenly the fog lifted, and I saw what was true—that my commitment to my children was *the only thing that mattered right now*. And there and then, I made a covenant with the Lord: that come what may, and no matter where Graham was and when, I would concern myself with the welfare of our kids, and I would trust the Lord to watch over us all. It sounds so simple to say it now. It was anything but simple at the time.

> *O God, you know my foolishness,*
> > *and my faults are not hidden from you.*
>
> *Let not those who hope in you be put to shame through me,*
> > *Lord God of hosts;*
> > *let not those who seek you be disgraced because of me,*
> > *O God of Israel.*
>
> *Psalm 69: 6-7*

Sixteen
A Larger Place

That's what we'd been hoping for, and that's what the Lord provided: s*everal* larger places, actually, but all in due season. The first was a bungalow in Coventry, belonging to some good folk named Booth. They, along with some members of their Baptist church, including the pastor, became intrigued with the "American experiment"—all these people from across the waters—us—and whatever it is that they—we—were doing. Maybe it was the sheer audacity of our *being* there that got their attention.

Clifford said one day, "Look, my house is not huge, but it's bigger than yours, and your whole *lot* would fit into it. *You* all move into our house, and we will move into yours."

Extraordinary, when you stop to think about it. Surely the Holy Spirit was at work here. It wasn't an offer we could, or did refuse. Our whole *lot* moved in there. Just as well, because another wave was headed our way from Houston. It was a wave of young adults from the parish who had been involved in the Way In coffeehouse and other outreach ministries of Redeemer Church, and seemed ready and willing for an overseas adventure. Our ranks were swelling.

Though the bungalow seemed palatial in comparison to 18 Milner Crescent, nine new arrivals, including one couple and their tiny son, filled it up in no time and once again we were "bulging at the seams." Why were all these folk needed, you might well ask? What Bishop Bardsley had seen in *Following the Spirit* was the kind of discipleship much needed in the English church, he told us. It was compelling to him to see a group of Christians living a lifestyle close enough to middle-class values that most church folk could identify with it, yet sacrificial enough to challenge them. Clearly it would take a sizeable number of us to transplant a sense of the life we had shared in Houston. Hence the wave.

We began to have weekly prayer-and-praise services in the ample lounge of the bungalow, inviting folk like Clifford and Heather Booth and others from their church plus members of our Anglican parish, St. Philips, plus neighbors. There were lively songs, times of testimony, good solid Bible teaching, and an opportunity for the laying-on of hands and healing prayers. We participated fully as parishioners in the life of St. Philips, though none of us was on staff; it was a parish of modest size. Already, invitations were coming for us to visit other churches, some of whose leaders had been at the diocesan conference and had seen the film. There was plenty to do. To counter-balance our own culture shock we seemed to be creating a bit ourselves. Occasionally when I went for a morning jog—a daily habit in Houston—I could see lace curtains being drawn back as curious housewives peered out to get a closer view.

"When in England, eat as the English do" became our mantra. We wanted the children to fit in, and this was a fairly obvious way to help them. We adopted a weekly menu at the Bungalow; it featured things like bangers and mash—English sausages and mashed potatoes—on one night, fish and chips on another night, Cornish "pasties"—little meat pies, but you'd have to look hard to find the meat—and baked potatoes with trimmings. I don't remember any serious complaints from the kids, but growing kids do get hungry. As for the adults in the household who were not part of the shopping and cooking team, they wouldn't have *dared* complain at this stage of the game. Their survival instincts were too strong.

Now I look back on Coventry as a landing-strip for our ministry in the U.K; but at the time it was all we had, all we could see with the naked eye. There were moments of awe when we first saw the amazing new Coventry Cathedral over-looking the ruins of the old. There were excursions to Kenilworth Castle and Stratford-on-Avon, the latter on a large English coach which took tour groups around. We were determined to expose the children to some of their Anglo heritage, and these enrichment opportunities kept us from getting too homesick for the *old country*—known to some as the *new world*. None of us qualified for work visas in the U.K. save Virginia, an experienced social worker. Within two months she had sailed through the qualifying process: the government had to be assured you had a skill they needed and were better qualified than any English worker. Ta-da. Now we were *really* fitting in.

We were fitting into the church scene, too, judging from the invitations that began to pour in. There were many churches eager to enliven their worship. Worship-leading skills were much less marketable than social work but nonetheless in demand. The best that could be expected by way of recompense was an offering and some help with travel expenses. But that was ok. None of us had signed on for the money. We soon realized that, unlike materialistic America where everything seemed to have a price-tag, the British frame of mind about spiritual ministry went something like this: after all, if it's spirit-inspired, it's free . . . right? So we accustomed ourselves to functioning within this framework, and trying to expand the thinking as time went on; for now, the ox was fairly well muzzled. That is not to say that there were not generous gestures of reaching out to us. One was especially meaningful to me: a group of church-women in the Coventry diocese found out ahead of time the ages and sizes of our children and hand-knitted sweaters for each of them by the time we arrived. That was awesome.

By April 1973 things were humming along, we had absorbed the nine new household members, and not only that. One traveling team could not possibly keep up with all the invitations for ministry, and we had been in touch with Houston to plead, "Send reinforcements." I think this was the period when some began to refer to Graham as the international harvester.

Anticipating another swell in ranks by early summer made the Bungalow inadequate to our housing needs. Once again a larger place was needed. We were also dealing with realities of making our way in a new land, not wanting to be a continuing financial drain on the Houston parish, but needing some time to get ourselves going over here. One day we noticed a banner which one of the Fisherfolk had made: it was a simple banner showing five loaves and two fish. A simple banner, but *made* for this very moment, because here we were, wondering how the Lord could feed all these folk who had come across the waters—ourselves included. We thought about that young lad who had quite simply offered Jesus his small lunch. It was all he had, but Jesus took it, blessed it, and the multitudes were fed—with twelve baskets left over. In reflecting on what this story meant for us in the here and now, we concluded that if *we* put what we had in the Lord's hands, just as the little boy did by offering his loaves and fishes, we *also* could expect wondrous results. So that is what we did. Many emptied savings accounts back in the States, each one praying about how the story applied to them. Here is one of the remarkable things the Lord did:

Virginia and I drove to the Cotswolds one day to view an old house in an estate sale. Friends had suggested it might make a roomy, more permanent home for us. On a picturesque, twisting village lane, whom should we see walking in the sunshine but Brother Anthony—a monk we had known at the Benedictine monastery in Michigan. What was he doing here in England, a continent away from where we had last seen him? He had every reason to be here, as it turned out, since Nashdom Abbey in Buckinghamshire was home to his Benedictine brothers in England. He was obviously visiting them, and as surprised to see us as we were to see him.

Sharing our ongoing quest for a larger place for our burgeoning ministry, he proceeded to describe a manor house in Berkshire with an old folks' wing attached—*déjà vu*. The brothers had pastoral oversight of the Sisters of the Good Shepherd, an order of nuns who were living there. They were a dwindling order with only three sisters remaining, and the Mother Superior was terminally ill with cancer. As stewards of the estate the brothers would have sole responsibility for it when the sisters were no longer in residence. They were on the lookout for potential new occupants for this enormous old Victorian manor house with its adjacent vineyards, rose gardens, and laundry block. Well, *here we were.* Virginia and I could hardly wait to get back to Coventry to share the exciting news. It had all the markings of one of those "God" moments: something you could not possibly have envisioned or engineered just waiting for you around a turn in the road.

And—it came to be. For one British pound sterling we were able to lease Yeldall Manor for a year. The Lord had really "done us proud" as they like to say in the south. At last we had enough room to do most anything, and certainly to house the young folk who had come from Houston. The ground was moving under our feet again. Adventures we had had to date pale by comparison to what awaited us at Yeldall.

But first . . . we had to get there. In stages, as it turned out, since the children were still finishing up their Coventry school year. Despite the story-book quality of Yeldall—the name comes from the elision of *Ye Old Hall*—there was much work needed to get it in habitable shape for us all. So a work-team of adults went down with scrub-brushes and pails in hand. First they decided to attack the annex, the old folks' wing, so that we could occupy that wing while work continued in the cavernous old house itself.

The Yeldall pioneering team really rolled up their sleeves and took charge of things down there. Graham was amongst them—no surprise there. When he was around there was never a lot of goofing-off. By the time the rest of us arrived six weeks later the wing was spit-polished, with no faint hint of nursing-home odor. Each of the small bedrooms had been set up, with linen on the beds and all the rest of it. Good job. But that wasn't all. The forerunner team had established a schedule for getting things done, and they folded the rest of us into their schedule with the greatest of ease.

Lyrics of an old World War I song came to mind: "You're in the army now, ta-da-da-da-da . . . . da-da." It was just like boot camp. I felt bemused and a little confused, but hey. It was working. A bell rang in the early morning—Graham had forewarned me about this—giving you fifteen minutes to get up, make your bed, wash your face or whatever, get dressed and be ready for the long trip down the hall as soon as the next bell sounded. The second bell was to announce that breakfast was being served in the dining room. So, before the sleep was thoroughly out of your eyes you had been launched into a new and productive life, whatever your mood of the moment might have been. Obviously, sleeping 'til noon was not one of the options.

It makes me laugh now, looking back, but at the time it was down-to-cases, serious stuff; like being led into the wilderness and given a few survival tools. Had the pioneering group *not* established a daily discipline for getting the necessary work done to make this house a home, heaven knows what would have happened to us. Now for the romantic part:

Yeldall truly *was* a storybook place. At every turn it conjured up images of a bygone Victorian era when landed gentry lived on estates like this, with a full complement of domestic servants to make possible life in the grand manner—while they were living *in* the grand manor. There had been cooks who tended the coal-fed *Aga* stove, praying for good winds to blow on the days they were roasting meat—otherwise dinner might turn into a midnight feast. There had been gardeners who tended the gracious flower beds including a rose garden clearly visible beyond the leaded-glass windows of the dining-room. This elegant room had a high ceiling, with a minstrels' gallery at one end where musicians could provide dinner music. Underneath there was a cozy nook with an inviting fireplace—the sort of place that just *begs* you to sit down for a little *natter* with a friend over a cup of tea. There most certainly would have been grounds-keepers on staff, to tend the world-class collection of trees and shrubs which the original owner had accumulated—a fabulous collection including an avenue of giant sequoias, cedars from the Himalayas, to mention a few. The builder/owner had been a world-traveler, and had managed to ship beautiful specimens home to his estate, creating his own wonderland, a place of stunning beauty to the eye.

Holidays were especially memorable at Yeldall. As Christmas approached we decked the halls, preparing for a genuine yuletide celebration. Mikel Kennedy was sent out to buy a Christmas tree. Approaching the vendor with a typically Texan request, he drawled, "Gimme the biggest tree you've got!" Well, he got it.

It was a twenty-foot tree, and it looked stunning in the elegant Yeldall dining-room. The only question was, how shall we decorate such an enormous tree? We had no Christmas decorations—*nada*. We were, after all, immigrants of a sort, or more accurately, adoptees. We certainly hadn't had room for Christmas decorations when we came across the waters. So this was going to be a challenge.

Virginia to the rescue. She rummaged around the manor house until she found lots of pretty little blue-and-white Delft pitchers which the nuns had conveniently left. Also, there were carved wooden spindles for making lace. Armed with these and a fertile imagination, she procured some wide gold organdy ribbon—lots of it. We tied the pitchers and spindles onto the tree with big organdy bows. We spotlighted the tree, and *voilà. Magnifique.* Perhaps most wonderful of all, somehow we felt we were carrying forward the history of the place God had provided for us to dwell in.

Day by day there were many chores to do to keep our home sparkling and inviting, or just plain clean. There were back-breaking jobs like those in the laundry, where our clothes were washed in big bathtubs of sudsy water, wrung by hand, then rinsed and dried on enormous wooden racks overhead. There were clever reminders from those assigned to clean the bathrooms, like: "Love never leaves an empty loo-roll."

Outside many of the guys and lads battled the nettles, clearing away all manner of weeds. In the kitchen life was busy, too. Big shopping excursions to a nearby farmers' market yielded healthy fruits and veggies. Preparing them for a dinner for fifty—at times sixty or more—was a time-consuming but rewarding job, made easier if the Aga behaved and the wind blew, providing necessary bellows for the coal to burn and the dinner to cook. Afterwards there were dishes to be done, and team-work needed to do it. There was one small dishwasher so the lion's share of the dishes was done by what we now call *sweat equity*. That's where you rolled up your sleeves, grabbed a dish-towel and didn't stop 'til the job was done. A guy named John was considered by all as the fastest, most efficient dishwasher on the planet.

Mentioning the figure *sixty* intimates that there had been a population explosion of sorts, since sixteen in the original Coventry group plus nine who came across in February 1973, plus nine more who followed before the Nottingham Conference *still* doesn't add up to sixty. If those are impressive numbers, consider the fact that trusted friends from those days assure me there were as many as 120 at the peak of it all. This counts, in addition to the manor house, those living in adjacent cottages and the Thatched House in Wargrave. That number seems to have slipped from my memory, but it must be true. These added numbers represented British families from a variety of church traditions, both Anglican and free-church, who hungered for more genuine community in their churches. Somehow—God only knows—we made them thirsty for this, and for experiencing the fruit of our life together. So they came, some of them single, some in families, but all with a similar quest. They were not looking to *join* our community; they were eager to *learn* from our experience of sharing and caring for one another. So they moved in with us for a time and joined in doing whatever we were doing, doing it *alongside* us.

Worship remained the focus of our life together: not a stylized formal type of worship, but the sort that drew us together in a rich sharing of our common humanity. The roots of this kind of worship had been planted back in Houston in things like daily Bible sharing at the church and the coffeehouse ministry, in both of which personal testimony was encouraged. What was the living Lord doing in our lives today? Some shared their testimony best through poetry and music, others would tell how a verse from Scripture had been brought alive in an everyday experience. On one occasion Maggie Durran came to a morning Bible sharing time with a new text she had written, based on the words of Isaiah the prophet: *Beautiful on the mountains are the feet of the bearer of good news!* The beauty of her poem so inspired me that I wrote a musical setting of it before the day ended, and shared it at our weekly Eucharist that night. This kind of synergy was at the heart and core of Celebration's creativity; a richly shared life simply bore rich fruit of the sort you cannot buy in a store.

At one point when Bey and Jane visited us in 1974, they arrived on a Saturday set aside as a community work-day. Friends from the area had been invited to come and help with deep cleaning and care of the grounds. Arriving in the front hall after their trans-Atlantic flight and before their suitcases had been set down, Bey and Jane were handed a rake by an eager foreman and given an assignment. *No messing around here.* The humor of the situation became apparent. Later, commenting on her Yeldall experience, my mother Bey was heard to say, "The folks back home in my Baptist church could understand the enlarged household at Redeemer in Houston. But . . ." she paused and shook her head slowly, "they'll *never* understand this."

There were particularized tasks, of course. Now that we had attracted the attention of Britain's prime publisher, *Hodder & Stoughton,* the professional musicians in our midst—chiefly Mimi Farra and myself—were hard at work editing and preparing compilations of songs and hymns for publication. This was clearly a part of the Lord's providing for us on these foreign shores. So we worked hard. The fruit of this work culminated in three published songbooks: *Sound of Living Waters, Fresh Sounds*—with Jeanne Harper as co-editor, *and Cry Hosanna!*— all published between 1974 and 1980. The books were well received in the U.K., and published all over the English-speaking world.

Yeldall Manor served our ministry purposes very well indeed. The location, close to major motorways, made travel accessible, and not infrequently two teams of young folk would be on the road simultaneously. Once in Chorleywood the local vicar was trying to introduce them. He said, "I want you to meet a team of young lay ministers from the Fishermen, Incorporated, from the Church of the Redeemer, from . . ."

Eyes were glazing over, so he gave up the lengthy intro and exclaimed, *"Greet these young Fisherfolk."*

And there it was. We had our name—the name first encountered in the anthem we had sung two years before on another continent. The only thing missing was the lapping of the waves, but we would be hearing them soon enough.

Ecclesiastically speaking, the Yeldall period represented a milestone. We were now resident in the Diocese of Oxfordshire, with a new bishop who just *happened* to be chaplain to all the Anglican religious orders. Thanks in part to a clarifying visit from Bishop Woolcombe, we were able to "see ourselves as others saw us." He reckoned that we were an experimental religious community and suggested we give ourselves a name. The name "Community of Celebration" was chosen, or revealed—in all likelihood to Graham himself. For there was no question that it was to Graham that the Lord had given an enormous vision of drawing together the body of Christ right where we were. It was a liturgical gift, in the broadest meaning of that word; it was the *people's work,* and he was the facilitator. He was integral to the ordering of our daily life of worship, work, and recreation. He could mastermind an elegant smorgasbord on holiday occasions; he could call a fast during Lent; he could teach a riveting Bible study or preach a good sermon. He could do and did all of these things, none seeming more important than the other, because he saw our life in its totality as the raw material out of which worship was made. His most oft-quoted verse in the Bible was from Romans 12: 1: *I appeal to you therefore, brothers and sisters, by the mercies of God, to present your bodies as a living sacrifice, holy and acceptable to God, which is your spiritual worship.* Worship was for Graham the presenting of our pluralities to God *as one.* So all of life was the content of worship. We celebrated this life when we came together for Eucharist; therefore *Celebration* was a fitting name for our gathered life. Over the years ahead we "traveled" with both this name and the more popular folk title *Fisherfolk.* The latter came to represent the outreach ministry, recordings and books of our gathered life, and *Celebration* represented the community life itself.

There were humorous touches to our life in the grand manor. Out of deference to our age and station in life—or *you* tell me what it was—Graham and I were assigned the master bedroom. That's the one at the end of the house with the high barreled ceiling and enormous windows overlooking the beautiful surrounds, the room with balcony attached and a fireplace at one end, and oh, yes—I almost forgot: it's the one which received whatever heat was left in the pipes after all the other rooms had received theirs. The antiquated heating system was one of the less glamorous features of this old house. Our friends meant well when they gave us such a plum of a room, but it was like being assigned to Siberia.

Not only that, but we were promoted to these quarters as soon as the room had been cleaned and prepared for occupancy, and the children were still in the wing—a football field away. I'll never forget the first night Graham and I stayed in that room. I went to bed armed with not one, but *two* hot-water bottles. Around midnight I roused slightly in the darkened room, and saw—some twenty-five feet away at the other end of the room, a shaft of light into the hallway. The door had been opened slightly, and two small pajama-clad figures stood there, silhouetted against the hall light.

"Mama?" "Daddy?" they inquired.

"Who's there?" said the big bad wolf.

Not really. It was Graham, his bass voice resonating in the half-empty room. Then we both saw Martha and David, our two youngest, who had come to check on us. They had made the long trek from the wing, through the main floor of the house, up the winding stairway, and down the hallway—to where they only *hoped* we were. They had done this in the middle of the night, with no adult chaperoning or guidance. They were missing us. The feeling was mutual, not to mention something else I was missing: our small heat-able room in the wing—the one we had left behind for these grander quarters.

The people we met while living at Yeldall were grander than the place itself. One was the Bishop of Buckinghamshire, an assistant bishop in our diocese, who had dinner with us one Saturday evening. We were in the habit of making Saturday dinners special, not only the food, but the after-dinner entertainment as well. Tonight the children were to perform one of their Winnie—the—Pooh plays. The good bishop seemed delighted. Earlier in his ministry, he told us, he had been the vicar of the church A.A. Milne attended, and had known Christopher Robin as a little boy. Wow!

The most memorable of all was an unexpected Sunday afternoon visitor. Community members were off hither and yon enjoying unscheduled time in a variety of ways. I happened to be the only person downstairs, so I answered the front door to see a beaming face and hear,

"Hello. I am Desmond Tutu, and this is my family. We are visiting Lord Remnant." Lord Remnant was the adjacent landowner. "We wanted to come over to greet you."

I invited them inside. In the cozy nook, beside burning embers in the small fireplace, we sat while he told of their approaching departure for South Africa, where he was to become the Anglican Dean of St. Mary's Cathedral in Johannesburg— the first black person to hold that position. Well aware of the seething unrest in his homeland and the challenges ahead, he asked for our prayers. I told him a bit about our odyssey and how we had come to be here. His wife and children were lovely. The whole experience is etched in gold in my memory, because—who could have known? Who could have dreamt that he would become one of the key figures in the bloodless revolution which overcame apartheid in his beloved country? To have met such a man at such a time I count as one of the choicest blessings of my life.

He was on his way to greatness—as the kingdom calculates it. We were on our way to—Scotland, as it turns out. Our lease at Yeldall would soon run out unless we renewed it or managed to purchase the property, which we had no means of doing. In the meantime there had been contact by several north-of-the border churchmen, one of whom had informed Graham of an existing need in the Scottish Church. The upshot of all of this was an invitation from Bishop Richard Wimbush, then Primate of the Scottish Episcopal Church. He invited us to come to Millport on the Isle of Cumbrae, Graham as Provost of the Cathedral of the Isles, and the community to occupy and care for the two attached college buildings. The big advantage here was an ecclesiastical appointment for Graham, which would be an anchor for us all. So, let me see—is the ground moving again under our feet? I think so.

Happy are the people whose strength is in you!
whose hearts are set on the pilgrims' way.
Psalm 84: 4

Seventeen
Another Land

Another dwelling-place awaited us in another land; but first we must cross the waters again—this time the English Channel and North Sea. Looking back now it seems obvious: Scandinavia was good preparation for Scotland. Since the time of the Vikings there had been a strong link between the two, both of them *north countries* geographically and temperamentally. We had been invited to a Swedish Lutheran conference center, *Stiftsgården,* at Rättvik. Nestled in Dalarna, the folk-center of Sweden, overlooking a beautiful lake, it was an ideal summer assignment. Leaving a group at Yeldall to prepare for the Scottish exodus, a sizeable number of us including one Fisherfolk team left for Sweden on a Swedish liner destined for Gothenburg.

The trip itself was memorable. We all got sea-sick. All, that is, except ex-Navy man Graham who had excellent sea-legs. Once during Navy days on his first ocean voyage aboard the submarine tender *Bushnell,* a violent storm had blown up near Cape Hatteras, N.C., a place notorious for shipwrecks in olden days. The captain of the ship had taken sick, likewise the second officer. The chain of command then became audible, and crucial to the survival of all: "Over to you, sir," would come orders to the next in line. Amazingly, there had been so many sick officers that the command finally fell to Graham, a Lieutenant, j.g. *who had never steered a ship before.* They all survived, but it made for good stories to tell your children.

There was at least one other sea-worthy person in our family as it turned out: ten-year-old Martha. She and her daddy and several team members actually made it to the elegant *Smorgasbord* that had been much touted and highly anticipated by us all. David and I ventured from our cabin and made it *almost* to the dining-room, then had to turn back. Woe is me, that is, *us*. Later someone told us the North Sea was noted for this kind of stormy weather. We heard glowing reports of the elegant food, but didn't want details: just pass the crackers, please.

Stiftsgården was full of new and enchanting experiences for us all. The habitual sauna followed by a jump in the cold lake was very new indeed. *Did I actually do that?* The picturesque old *kyrka* was the setting for our worship services including Saturday evening prayers which I recall as a meaningful preparation for Sunday's liturgy. There was little doubt that we were in the folk-heart of Sweden because every other person seemed to be carving a piece of wood into something beautiful or useful or both. *Then there was the food,* so distinctive and delicious. There were fish of many sorts, cultures like *filmjölk,* luscious lingonberries, mild chilled a*ppelsoppa,* a fruit soup for dessert, and incredible breads, mildly sweet, which we called *limpa brod.*

In preparation for our family summer in Sweden we had engaged the help of several Swedish visitors at Yeldall. At dinner they would teach us how to ask for things like *smöret*—that being one that sticks in my head like a stick of butter—which it is. By the time we arrived in Sweden we were functional at the dinner table, but nowhere else. Our limited vocabulary revolved around getting our stomachs fed. Not only that: most Swedish folk under age fifty were proficient in English and highly motivated to use it, leaving us minimal opportunity to practice our limited Swedish. *C'est la vie,* as they say in that other country whose language I *had* studied. This was most definitely not France.

It wasn't England either, and the Nordic difference was hard to miss. Swedes I met seemed to have a particular gift for *melancholy,* finding expression in their songs and poetry—must be all those long winters and the shortage of sunshine. So different than warm countries south of the U.S. border with much dancing and singing and playing of folk instruments outdoors, where young and old draw together around village squares. Here the Scandinavian temperament seemed to seek solace from the elements by going inside. Those long winter nights offer much time to brood over lost loves or life in general. Surely, climate is part of the difference. I was grateful for a summer's exposure to the Swedish temperament, and it proved fruitful in enriching our community life: Years have passed since then and there are still many enduring relationships. One of the most significant bonds was the marriage of Ruth, one of the Fisherfolk and a gifted artist, to Håkan, a Swedish priest and widower with four children. How wondrous are God's ways.

On to Scotland, *sans* Graham, as it turned out. He needed to fly to the States for medical consultations following some cardiovascular symptoms. Ever since our trip down-under earlier that year I had been harboring a concern for his heart health. Mostly it was intuitive, but I had read an article that troubled me. It said the appearance of deep creases in the earlobes could be indicative of heart trouble. I had recently noticed those— something that seemed new in Graham's appearance, and I had mentioned it to him. The response was the usual deflection of wifely concerns that sounded so familiar.

But now, I *really* felt concerned. We needed to get the children to Scotland in time for school to begin, so it was a relief that Bill Farra could fly to the States with Graham, while Mimi and I accompanied the three younger children on the homeward journey—to a home as yet unseen. We drove across scenic Norway, enjoying views of dramatic mountain peaks and deep fjords, occasionally glimpsing one of those darling mountain-goats who have suction cups attached to their paws—else, how could they spring with such ease from craggy bluff to craggy bluff? *En route* we spent the night in a fairly typical coastal-town hotel learning to thank God for elevators, as there were none here and our rooms were on the fourth floor, *a long way up*.

This time our North Sea and Channel crossing was on a large English ferry, and the weather was calmer. But *shucks,* no Smorgasbord. Instead we were back to beans on toast, bangers and mash and typical English fare. We were headed for Scotland, where the cuisine leans more in a continental direction, which is to say, tastier. Landing in Newcastle-on-Tyne we drove across England, northwards into Scotland, to the coastal town of Largs on the Firth of Clyde. The deep tones of twilight were there to meet us, but there was something else as well. I could hear the music again.

Standing on the ferry slip awaiting our crossing to the Isle of Cumbrae, I heard the lapping waves at water's edge, bringing back the mystical musical *motif* from Houston days, the one that had morphed into the *Fisherfolk* anthem. I was hearing in stereo, one ear listening to the small rippling waves I could see, the other tuned into that music that had traveled across the world to meet me. They had finally come together: the lapping waves and the music. They had met together as one. It was a holy moment for me, a *thin place* before I knew the term. It was too deeply moving for me to speak about just now—with kids in tow, and our new home at the Cathedral yet to find. Besides, the ferry would stop running soon. There were no evening crossings of the Clyde. So we hastened on to the island.

It was a short ferry ride—about fifteen minutes, and also a short ride from the ferry slip into the town of Millport. The evening shadows were lengthening by the time we arrived. The spire of the Cathedral would surely stand out against the dimly lit sky, so we looked for that. *"There it is,"* one of the kids yelled. We followed the lead, and drove up to—sure enough—an old building with a real spire. As we got closer our hearts sank.

"Could this be the Cathedral?"

"Look at all the busted windows. It's worst than the East End of Houston."

"Graham never mentioned that the building was derelict . . ."

"Well, we'll just have to find out," said I in my most hopeful voice, trying to reassure the children. We pulled up to what looked like a residence next-door to the Cathedral. Mimi went to inquire and was met at the door by a kindly and oh-so-Scottish face. It was the local potter Donald Swan, who explained that this was a de-commissioned Church of Scotland building which he and his wife Elizabeth had taken over and converted into a pottery. They lived next-door in the Manse. Whew.

"And can you tell us where we might find the Cathedral of the Isles?" Indeed he could, and indeed he did. And indeed we went there as fast as our little legs would carry us—though still a bit weak in the knees from this turn of events.

If that statement about our little legs carrying us sounds like a fairy tale, here's why. A true confession follows. The things I have just told you are in essence true, that *is* the way I remembered them, but my memory merged *two* episodes into one. I now know there were actually two arrivals in Scotland—one in March 1975 when a few of us traveled up to Millport for Graham's installation as Provost of the Cathedral. *That* was when I heard the lapping waves and the Fisherfolk music again, and *that* is when we drove to the "wrong" spire and met the Swanns who directed our path in the way that we should go. At our second coming to Cumbrae, with children in tow, we were able to drive directly to our destination. A much smoother transition for the kids, but the confabulated version makes a better story. *Mea culpa* . . .

Life in Scotland turned out to be surprisingly different from life in England. On the map they look so snug and close, the two of them plus Ireland fitting into the square footage of the United States thirty-seven times over. My grandson Liam did the math. But appearances can be deceiving, and despite the fact of their geographical closeness and the name *United Kingdom*, it was sometimes hard to spot the united bits. History has a lot to do with that, I'm sure. From this north-of-the-border perspective, most of the money and clout seem to flow towards London, and the Scots were basically regarded as country cousins of the English aristocracy, or downright non-conformists.

Consequently, the educational systems took off from a different point of view, even or especially in the case of young children. I remember the jovial Welsh headmaster at Knoll Hill Infant School in Berkshire; on the first day of school he assured us that Jane, Anna, Martha, Carl and David—our younger three and Virginia's younger two—would be well cared for at his school. "We may not have the highest academics in the country, but I can tell you that Knoll Hill will be a happy experience for your children. That is what is important at this age." We agreed. Such a gentle approach, so nurturing.

Not so in Scotland, where you land on your feet and better get going, *whatever* age you are. "Pull up your sox, laddie, on y'er bicycle." is a typical Scottish admonition to youngsters, convincing them that, as the poet had it, *"Life is real, and life is earnest . . . "* If you consider yourselves in any way underlings in a society, then you must work hard, struggle to succeed, not take anything for granted. Standing on your feet was not mere rhetoric, but a classroom discipline applied daily to expose the unprepared or timorous in spelling or in mental arithmetic. Those who arose too slowly might get their ears tweaked. Just think: this highly competitive approach has produced many outstanding scholars, inventors, and authors. As I look back on our years in the U.K., I am grateful that my children were exposed to *both* approaches.

One conflict arose with a Scottish school official when Martha was eleven years old and confined at home with severe tonsillitis. She had been through round after round of antibiotics to get the infection under control so she could have her tonsils removed. The medical merry go round lasted for months. I had contacted the headmaster to get Martha's assignments, hoping she could keep up with her class. We were blessed by the presence of a New Zealand teacher—now an Anglican priest—who worked diligently with Martha to help her with her academics. The missing ingredient was any contact with her classmates, her friends at school. Martha was such a *people* person. I went to have a chat with the headmaster and explained our dilemma, hoping he might help. My fatal mistake was mentioning America. Just by way of example I told him,

"Back in the states, when a child is out of school for a very long time, the classmates will sometimes write a note of encouragement to them and the teacher will send it—a sort of get-well message, I guess." He was not amused.

"Mrs. Pulkingham," he said stiffly, "when Martha has successfully completed her surgery, *then* her classmates will send her a note to congratulate her." His words stung my ears. *You mean, even for a sick child, it's still all about success? You unfeeling, tyrannical man,* I thought, and went home sadly.

Once again, music was the key that unlocked many joyful experiences on the island. The elderly music teacher at the Cumbrae School fell ill and was no longer able to teach. The school knew of the Community's musical skills and turned to us for help. My musical companion Max Dyer and I would go several times a week to the school. He with cello in hand and I at the piano would teach simple folksongs to the children and engage them with the joy of making music together.

With springtime in view, we realized the school was accustomed to end-of-term *finales*. A musical seemed ideal. We devised one, drawing on Celebration's repertoire of songs for children and Patricia Beall's dramatic skills to write the libretto. Our production, *Put on your Boots* took its name from the theme-song, and was sub-titled *A Musical Journey through the Centuries:*

> *Come with me to a land where people are free,*
> *Where the lambs and the wolves roam together through the country,*
> *They say that a child can ride on a lion's back,*
> *And not one man steals food from his brother's shack.*
> *(Refrain)*
> *So put on your boots, let's get on the road,*
> *There's just not that much time, you know.*[4]
>
> Sherrell Prebble, 1971

---

[4] Sherrell Prebble, Copyright 1971, 1975, Celebration.

It was a journey of faith, hearkening back to the time of Abraham, father of the faithful. Each class had its own production number, and no two of them were alike. *Samuel* was performed with a puppet show; *Joshua Fit the Battle of Jericho* was staged with big boxes as the walls, and eager student "soldiers" marching 'round Jericho. A slide-show featured our own island potter, Donald Swann, accompanied by the singing of *Jeremiah, Go Down to the Potter's House*. I don't know who was having more fun: the kids or the producers.

The Scottish audience proved enthusiastic as well. These were days before anyone made a fuss about religious themes in schools. In Scotland and England in the seventies it was not a problem. The Judeo-Christian roots of this community were a given; they were just *there*, in the same way as those "old eternal rocks" which St. Patrick memorialized in his famous hymn.

Scotland was for me a new cradle of creativity. The *mystique* of the western isles enveloped you in unavoidable ways. Living on a small island brought a sense of focus, of isolation; living here made me *want* to write music. In England I had spent much time arranging songs for various songbooks and hymnal supplements. Here I had more time to drink deeply from the wells of inspiration and create new music. Much of it was geared for usefulness in our Cathedral of the Isles worship: responsorial psalm settings, anthems, hymns, special liturgical settings such as the *Exsultet*. Who could have imagined that this small cathedral with its exquisite acoustics would become our recording studio— for *years?* It was a sheer gift from a gracious God.

Of course, the beauty of sounds that emanated from those recording sessions did not tell the whole story. There was no effective heating system in the Cathedral, so we came to those sessions wrapped up in our warmest clothing. Those who had to play musical instruments carried hot-water bottles. We had been prepared for this Spartan endeavor simply by *living* in the Cathedral compound—either *North College* or *South College*. It took all the fortitude I could muster to undress myself once a week in an ice-cold bathroom for a hot tub bath.

At one of our earliest community meetings in the Common Room, a member asked, "How do we go about getting in touch with the culture of Scotland? How do we learn what it's like to be Scottish? I mean, when we lived in Berkshire we could drive over and attend Evensong in Windsor Chapel, and get a real feel for things English . . ."

After a thoughtful pause, Lady Faith Lees who was visiting from Dorset, said, "Oh, I think you *are* getting into feeling Scottish already. I see you braving the gales outside to fill your buckets with coke to keep the little fireplaces going. This is *very* Scottish. This is what the Scots have been doing for centuries."

So much for nice romantic images of England. Here, life was real and life was earnest. Make no mistake. That became unavoidably clear on one Sunday afternoon in February 1976, when a fire erupted in North College. Most of us were attending an afternoon event in the Cathedral. Only two people were in the College at the time: one was Bill Farra who was ill, and the other was Mikel and Carol Kennedy's baby son Jeremy who was napping. Bill was able to rescue Jeremy and carry him to safety before the entire building was gutted with smoke—as we watched in horror.

The island fire department had arrived, of course, but the hoses leaked and there was no water pressure adequate to the task. More than half the community members lost all that they had brought from the States, which wasn't a lot. We were grief-stricken. In the days that followed, however, we began to see God's merciful hand at work.

> *God's purposes will ripen fast, unfolding every hour;*
> *The bud may have a bitter taste, but sweet will be the flower.*
> William Cowper, 1731-1800

The flower which began to unfold was the flower of mercy which grew in the hearts of the stalwart islanders, who until now had not been amused or enamored by this group of mostly Americans. We had seemed to them an invading presence; now we were needy souls lacking food and shelter. Bridges of friendship began to be built as a direct result of this ravaging fire.

In order to enter fully into the life of the island we needed to identify with its depressed economy and become productive citizens of Millport. The local bakery, a real hub and daily gathering place, was on the verge of going out of business. Three Celebration members offered to go to baking school in Glasgow for a three-year course condensed into two. Two of the three trained as bakers, and one in confectionary arts.

Entering into the life of this Scottish community was more than economics; it was aesthetics, too. Once when my friend George Mims was visiting from Houston, we had the great privilege of meeting and talking with Herbert Howells, the famous British composer. I recall telling him of my frustration with being on an island so cut off from the cultural mainstream. I was asking his help; how could I bring the beauty of the arts into this small island community? His response was immediate: "Start a choral society," he said. He spoke the word, and the Lord did the rest. The *Cumbrae Choral Society* was born—a wonderful blending of folk who loved to sing. The chief participants were members of the local Scottish *kirk* and our own lot from the Cathedral. Over the next few years we sang our way through the seasons: with the Christmas portions of Handel's *Messiah*, later the Easter portions of same, and then our real *tour d'force*, Mendelssohn's *Elijah*. We took certain liberties here—adapting the ambitious work to our available resources by substituting the spoken word at points to keep the continuity of the narrative. One memorable moment captured the fury of Israel unleashed against the prophet Elijah. In a dramatic choral reading full of Scottish *burrs* the male voices thundered forth: "Let the guilty prophet PER-R-R-ISH!"

It was enough to send cold chills down any spine. Besides all this, there was yet another musical on our agenda: this one generated by the Fisherfolk, designed for performance at the Edinburgh Festival Fringe in 1976. We performed it on consecutive nights over a two-week period at Old St. Paul's Church in Edinburgh. It was a great adventure, with good audience response. We were asked to bring the musical across the waters to Minneapolis during the Episcopal General Convention that summer, staging it at Gethsemane Church near the Convention center, where it ran for several nights. A tough assignment since the staging had to be taken down after each show so the church could be used for scheduled services the next day. Then the show had to be re-set for that night. Fortunately for our little troupe fresh from Scotland, we had reinforcements from our sister-community in Colorado* who were willing to serve as roadies. Without them we would have faced an impossible task.

All of this high-level exposure was launching us more and more onto a world stage. Were we ready?

> *Wake up, my spirit;*
> *awake, lute and harp;*
>   *I myself will waken the dawn.*
> *I will confess you among the peoples, O Lord;*
>   *I will sing praise to you among the nations.*
>   *Psalm 57: 8-9*

* In 1975 a group from Redeemer Church moved to Colorado at the invitation of Bishop Bill Frey, and set up a base for ministry at Woodland Park. A conference ministry developed there, enhanced by the natural beauty of this property located in the shadow of Pike's Peak. The community was in residence there from 1975—1985, the same decade during which the overseas community lived on Cumbrae Island in Scotland.

Eighteen
To The Ends Of The Earth

Music could go further than our legs could carry us. The music that evolved from our shared life—first at Church of the Redeemer, Houston, and later in the UK—this music somehow *carried* the life with it in a remarkable way. When people listened to our music, they felt invited into the life and made welcome there. The life and music were for us inseparable. Somehow it didn't feel right to be "marketing" our music in places where our faces had never been seen. So eventually we put a great deal of effort into ministering and traveling in places like South Africa, in countries down under, and throughout the entire English-speaking world.

If the recorded music ushered us onto a worldwide stage, it was produced in a hidden-away and unlikely spot. The isolation of our island home in Scotland was ideal for bringing focus to the work at hand, but the weather conditions were daunting. In a letter to my mother and Aunt Jane, dated February 17, 1976, I said:

> *Dear Bey and Jane, thank you for staying on your knees all week! And please thank Jim and Joyce for their prayers too. I can assure you they were much needed and the Lord honored them mightily.*
>
> *When we arranged the recording for the second week of February I sensed from the Lord that there would be obstacles*

to overcome, having to do with the weather particularly, because we are still in the midst of the tempestuous Scottish winter. Then two weeks ago, when we had a four-day storm and the roar of the wind in the Cathedral was deafening—plus the sound of tiles clacking on the roof and many of them blowing off, well, then I knew it was serious business about these winter gales. The week following was sunny and pleasant for the most part. Then on Monday, 10 February, the day Ray Prickett* was to arrive here, the ferries were cancelled because of the rough water, and the weather bureau reported that, with the exception of a lull between midnight and 6am there would be gale-force winds, and the same was predicted for the following day. (That meant gales for Tuesday and Wednesday, the first two days of the recording.)

By the afternoon, however, the ferries began to run and Ray was able to get across safely. That night I awoke at 3 am and could hear the wind rattling my window and the plastic covering over the window-pane. The "lull" must be over, I thought. I lay there listening to the wind and talking to the Lord for about ten minutes . . . as did others, I found out later. And, just as quickly as the wind had come, it ceased, as if directed by a heavenly hand. And I felt the Lord saying in that very moment, "The wind is mine, and it will go where I direct it." Do you know that in spite of the gale forecasts, we had clear calm weather for every hour of recording time . . . ? Thank you again for praying!

Early on in Scotland one of the community members shared a vision with us all: it was a beautiful flower closing its petals. Puzzling? As we prayed about how this vision related to us, the interpretation took shape: From our *Grand Central Station* life at Yeldall Manor in the throbbing heart of England, we had been drawn away to a different sort of place. Here life was more basic. There were still many chores to do, and added adventures such as picking bramble berries in season. But we were no longer thronged with visitors non-stop. There was more time to reflect, to create. And there was more time to deepen our life of worship and experience firsthand the balance of worship, work and study which the Benedictine order had practiced for years. We were—as the saying goes—*living into* a Benedictine way of life.

By and large, the same people who did the singing and playing on recordings also did the kneading and baking at Speirs Bakery, which we had purchased in 1977. Only a few of us were set aside for full-time work in the business of music, which was by this time truly a business. Not a glitzy business, as much religious music was becoming back in the States, but at least a business that brought in some financial support for our Community, and was fully expressive of our shared life.

The Cathedral of the Isles made an exquisite recording studio. Armed with blankets and hot water bottles, we would work for several hours at a time recording prepared songs and hymns and anthems, while our afore-mentioned, highly skilled recording engineer, listened from the "control room"—known to most as the church sacristy. Ray had long experience recording in churches—especially organs. He loved the live acoustic environment, and so did we. Our little three-rank organ was nothing to write home about if you were trying to say something *good,* but most of what we recorded did not rely primarily on the organ. The small cathedral literally *sang* for you, so perfect were the acoustics. Once in a while, as we put on that extra pair of heavy socks, wool gloves, and went in to sing, we may have been vaguely aware that the whole English-speaking world was listening. But all we *really* knew was that we were called by the Lord to do this, as part and parcel of our ministry. It would be years before we became aware of how deeply this music was touching lives all around the globe.

Meanwhile, the closed petals of the flower were regaining strength, being nurtured in the tough rich soil of Scotland and its Celtic heritage. We could gaze out from the Isle of Cumbrae and see through the mist the rugged shape of *Ailsa Craig*, the enormous rock which legend has it St. Patrick threw at the Devil. That rock lay halfway between Ireland and Scotland. Living as we did on a small island was like being tossed into the middle of *St. Patrick's Breastplate:*

> *I bind unto myself today the virtues of the starlit heaven, the glorious sun's life giving ray, the whiteness of the moon at even, the flashing of the lightning free, the whirling wind's tempestuous shocks, the stable earth, the deep salt sea, around the old eternal rocks.*
>
> Words attr. to St. Patrick (372-466)

St. Patrick had gazed on this massive rock as he wrote that last line, I feel sure. And here we were, centuries later, gazing at it too, drawing strength from the saints of yore. Especially was I drawn to the story of St. Columba. As we prepared music for publication, his story reminded us of the days before our intricate copyright laws, the days when the underlying principle of those laws was established in the simple dictum: "To every cow belongs her calf, and to every book her son-book."

Our publishing ventures had begun back in Houston where I sometimes could be found sketching melodies and words on the back of an order of service for an eager worshipper to take home, because they just *had to have this music*. Soon we had compiled *Songs of Fellowship,* which was an in-house publication of Redeemer Church. Before long we had been approached by the Gregorian Institute of America, who wanted to publish much of our music. Now, in the UK, a fruitful relationship developed with *Hodder & Stoughton,* whose gifted editor Edward England guided us into publishing a set of songbooks starting in the mid seventies. *Sounds of Living Waters* was first, followed by *Fresh*

Sounds, then *Cry Hosanna!* They were hymnal supplements, really, designed to capture some of the contemporary worship sounds, the new song settings that were cropping up all over the place, and many "right where we were"—to borrow a line from one of Diane Davis Andrews' well-known songs.

Right where we are is where I had stayed for a long time. Graham had been the one who did the traveling, while I kept the home fires burning. That dated back to Houston days and his first trip of great length and distance: to New Zealand. The miles had seemed forever—he was halfway around the world from where I stood in the supermarket and gazed down into the big blue eyes of our two-year old David. *"Though I go ten thousand miles . . . "* no longer seemed a quaint poetic phrase with a haunting tune. I felt every one of those miles. Graham would send cassette tapes to keep me informed, and would phone once a week; but knowing the cost-per-minute of these transoceanic calls made me tongue-tied. Everything that came to mind seemed too trivial to talk about at that price. Or it was too deep for a brief conversation. So I was an inept transoceanic phone companion.

Once we had lived in the UK for a while, Graham began to say to me, "You and your ministry need more exposure. You have a remarkable ministry in your own right. The Lord wants more people to benefit from it." At first I didn't give it much thought. But he was persistent once an idea struck him, so he kept reminding me of his impressions about this. And in due season they came to pass. The trip across to General Convention in the USA in 1976 was a harbinger of these things, but their unfolding happened after we actually moved back to the states in 1980.

Graham had become increasingly concerned about the parish back in Houston. Although he was no longer rector, there were deep bonds of affection with folk there, and he cared when he saw what looked like renewal running amuck, one symptom being a pushy lay leadership lacking due respect for the ordained ministry. Somehow the problem had not been so formidable during his tenure as rector—although I am the one pointing that out—he certainly never did. This was probably because Graham himself was not easily pushed around. In any case, back we went in 1980, along with three community members who volunteered to go with us to make up our household. Heaven help us. Some who had revisited Redeemer in recent times reported widespread frustration on the part of many who had moved there to "live out the dream of renewal" in this now-famous church. When their dreams did not materialize and pastoral problems abounded, they felt angry. Of course, now that we were coming back, what better target for their anger than the guy who had begun the whole deal? He was fairly well set up to become the guru in the road who needs killing.

In order that I could continue my work with research and development of worship resources, a little office was set up for Celebration Services in the beloved basement of Redeemer Church. I say beloved because it was just down the hall from the choir room where I had spent some of the happiest hours of my life as director of the parish choir in years gone by. Now was different, but good. Over the next year I helped produce a new recording of songs harvesting another crop of creativity from the parish. The Lord sent me the helper I needed in the person of Kevin Hackett, an incredibly gifted young man who was a musician and business-man: a jack of all trades and master of most.

Returning to any parish as its ex-rector is bound to be awkward, and Redeemer Church with its extraordinary history was no exception. The parish welcomed us warmly and provided a house in the neighborhood for us to live in. That was all well and good, but how was Graham to function? I'm not sure anyone knew precisely. According to Jeff Schiffmayer, who was rector at the time, Graham served as a *pastoral consultant.* One aspect of this that I know about is this: he spent time being a sounding board for some of those frustrated people who were waiting for their spiritual dreams to come true there. Undoubtedly, he encouraged some to get on with their lives and not wait for miracles to happen as in days of yore. This likely flew in the face of the parish leadership's desire to hang onto people and in some sense *emulate* the days of yore. Unfortunately—and Graham knew this—such emulation could easily morph into idolatry. The truth is: I knew very little about all the pastoral concerns of the moment; I was on another track, working hard on the music and traveling ministry parts of our lives.

1981 was the date of my first big overseas ministry trip. In the company of two Celebration members—both of them British—we went to Australia at the invitation of the Anglican Bishop of Canberra, who had visited the Houston church some years ago. He was organizing a Seminar on Church Music for his diocese, and wanted me and Celebration to be involved. Aside from the fact that they had their seasons upside down and talked with a twangy accent, those Aussies turned out to be nice folk. While we were there, a woman from Brisbane, an ardent Christian, approached us about sending a team of Fisherfolk to tour the urban centers of Australia, and offering herself to be our tour guide and organizer. Myra Wilkinson was sent from heaven, there is absolutely no doubt. Without her guidance and superb organizational skills such an ambitious tour could have been a fiasco. With her it was great joy. 1983 was the date of this return visit, this time with a team of eight.

But in the two intervening years, much happened on the ground. Graham had a life-threatening heart attack, followed by four way bypass surgery. He had been visiting friends in Denver when this happened, so the surgery took place there as well, and our household members came from Houston *en masse*. This was because Graham's primary-care doctor, a family practice man, was a firm believer in families *being* together at such crisis moments, both for the patient's sake and for their own. The surgery was successful and Graham returned to Houston. However, it was obvious he needed a change of pace, less stress in his life, more exercise, a stricter diet—all things any good cardiologist would recommend. So . . . what did we do?

We moved to Woodland Park, Colorado, with an altitude that would require oxygen for Graham to survive. Now, we didn't go there immediately—we weren't *completely* nuts—but within a year we were on our way to spend some time with the Celebration community in residence there.

A more picturesque setting would be hard to imagine. Located near the foot of Pike's Peak, the natural beauty of the area with its aspen woodlands was breathtaking. Grace Church, Colorado Springs, had established a summer retreat center here, which was now winterized and very comfortable. The Bishop of Colorado, known to us simply as Bill Frey, had been a friend to our ministry since early Redeemer, Houston days. His visits to the community were eagerly anticipated, as he was a brilliant liturgist and celebrant at Eucharistic feasts.

The Colorado setting provided yet another good rehearsal venue as our Fisherfolk team prepared for its big tour of Australia and New Zealand. Graham, of course, stayed behind, content to be "tucked away" in Woodland Park while I traveled forth with the Fisherfolk. He knew he had done all he could in Houston at this time, and that his recovery called for something fairly low-key at the moment. That worked for awhile, but by 1984 the altitude was proving difficult for his cardiac health. Also there were some big questions to be addressed about Celebration's future in the U.K. Was the Isle of Cumbrae in Scotland the place the Lord intended the community to dwell in perpetuity? What about the Celebration members who had gone south to Dorset to link up with the Post Green Community there? What did their future hold? As time elapsed and the Scottish community delved deeper into exploring the history and development of religious orders, more questions surfaced about long-term location.

My own experience of all this shuttling back-and-forth between USA and UK was far from theoretical. It hit me at gut level. Our youngest son, David was just getting started in high school, in Colorado, and moving back to the UK was bound to be disruptive to his education. However, I helped him pack his bags and depart with Graham, knowing the rest of us would join as soon as the traveling ministry schedule permitted. Their first stop was in Florida with Ran Chase and his family. Ran was a priest we had known at Kanuga and other outreach spots. Now he did an extraordinary thing: on their way to the airport where David and his dad were to board a plane for London, he invited David to stay in Florida and live with his family, in order to complete his high school education stateside. Graham's response had been, "Well, we'll have to see what Betty says . . ."

Betty almost dropped the phone when she heard this latest development. Somehow I could not imagine being separated from David—who was, after all, my *baby*—so abruptly and for several *years*. To help me absorb the shock of it all and see our way forward, I gathered the household members together quickly to talk—a kind of "group consciousness" meeting, while Graham and David and Ran held the phone in Florida and waited for the verdict. Our daughter Jane was visiting from University of Edinburgh at the time and proved invaluable, since she knew the British education system well, having been a part of it since age nine.

"Mom," she said, "David will be set back at least one, possibly two years in school if he goes back to Britain now. The 'O' levels and 'A' levels of the British system just do not mesh easily with the American high school system. It would be very disheartening to him."

I tried to let this sink in, and then I asked David—still on the line from Florida—how *he* felt about this plan.

"Mom," he said, "I think it will be the best thing for me. Ran says he can get me a scholarship at St. Andrews' School, where he is the chaplain, and I'll be just like a member of his family while I'm here."

So that did it. My body still felt wracked with grief and shock, but I could hear from the voices around me, and from David's own dear voice, that this was the way the Lord had opened up for him. And at the eleventh hour quite literally, as they were all set to board their international flight to the U.K., they pulled

David's suitcase off the conveyer belt and Graham boarded the plane alone. David went home with Ran. How extraordinary.

> *Although they have no words or language,*
> *and their voices are not heard,*
> *Their sound has gone out into all lands,*
> *and their message to the ends of the world.*
> *Psalm 19: 3-4*

* Ray Prickett, a sound engineer extraordinaire, recorded all of Celebration's albums in the U.K., as well as traveling to the States for several recordings. At the time mentioned in the letter (February 1976) the following were recorded: *Songs from Fresh Sounds* and *Worship with the Fisherfolk,* the latter proving to be the Fisherfolk's most popular recording.

Nineteen
Home Again

Excitement at seeing faraway places and exhilaration at meeting Christians in other cultures had expanded my world. So many people had *come home* with me through their songs, their laughter, the warmth of their hospitality and giving of themselves: the very smiles on their faces. Now, the prospect of moving back to the States and into a depressed urban town hit me like a dash of cold water.

This was true despite the fact that I had been fully a part of Celebration's 1984 discussions about the timeliness of relocating the community. There were several reasons it made sense: We needed to be close to an international airport to facilitate traveling ministry. We needed to be close to a seminary because some members desired more theological education and training. *And . . .* we needed to be in a place—yet again—where we could live out our commitment to be a friend to the poor and oppressed. The era of the flower folding its petals inward was over; the vision had borne fruit, and now it was time to move on. But where? That was the question. And why were my head and my heart so far apart?

For the past five years, Graham and I and members of our household had been in a truly itinerant ministry—dashing about the world here and there. So in many ways I could see the wisdom of the proposed move, if we could just find the right place, and the right bishop. Those two ingredients began to fall into place when we first met Alden Hathaway, then Episcopal Bishop of the Diocese of Pittsburgh. During a weekend of ministry in his diocese he turned to me rather impetuously and asked,

"Tell me . . . what would it take to get a group like Celebration to come live in my diocese?" I remember taking a deep breath, and saying something like,

"Well, I wouldn't say it would be easy, but—who knows? Stranger things have happened." That was about as hopeful but non-committal as I could sound. Truth to tell, I didn't have a clue what it would take, except that it was probably a lot more involved than he could imagine.

Now, some months later, he *was* inviting us to come, and it was serious enough that Graham and Bill Farra went over to "spy out the land" and see if there were a place and situation suitable for us. Aliquippa is what they found. A depressed, dying—or was it already dead and waiting for the death-wagon?—Steel town, one of the small communities ravaged by racial rage following the assassination of Martin Luther King, Jr. That was a scar that had never healed, so much so that many folk in the area were terrified even to drive through Aliquippa. The good news for us was that it was fifteen minutes from Pittsburgh's International Airport, and just across the Ohio River from Trinity Episcopal School for Ministry. *Voilà.* All three criteria fell into place, and we began to pack our bags for another great adventure.

As in the case of moving to Scotland via Sweden, we did not go directly there, but instead sent a Fisherfolk team ahead on a kind of re-entry to the USA tour, mostly to places up and down the east coast. At one point I happened to be in Houston for a few days; it was good to walk around those old familiar blocks near the church in the East End. That neighborhood and our life there had been a watershed of spiritual growth for me. But my heart was heavy as I thought forward to what it meant actually to *live* in Aliquippa. Compared to the nice parishes we had been visiting—many of whom had been or would become supporters and companions of Celebration, the "on the ground" reality of life in Aliquippa seemed at this point in time dismal to me. One clergyman in the Pittsburgh diocese had described the church's efforts there as "pouring resources into a black hole."

So I walked those Houston blocks in a fair amount of desperation, hoping against hope that in this place where I had found so much inspiration in the past, I might find it again. Here is what rose from the mist of memories:

There was nothing in his appearance that would attract us, there was no beauty that we should desire him . . .

These were the words of the prophet Isaiah concerning the Messiah. Slowly they sank into my conscious mind. This suffering servant, this Jesus, was in Aliquippa waiting for me. He *was* Aliquippa for now, for me. He was beckoning me to come, to be willing to be there with him for the sake of this hurting place. Would I follow him there? From that moment forward, Aliquippa looked different to me—through the new lens the Holy Spirit had provided. I turned my face in that direction, confident that the same Spirit who had given me the new look at Aliquippa would give me renewed strength for the living of these days. I would need every bit of that strength.

Celebration purchased a set of row houses on Franklin Avenue, the main thoroughfare through Aliquippa. The houses were available at fire-sale prices. These had been the sturdy, humble homes of one-time steel—workers who had kept the town buzzing and alive. Aliquippa had been a one-horse town, and the horse, named '*steel*', had died. The closing of the mills spelled economic doom for the town. Most of the workers had been trained in no other skills; many were in their late fifties, not expecting to launch out in a new direction. Not only that, their houses were for most their only investment, and who would buy their houses if they relocated to find work? *No one.* It was a bleak picture.

Celebration certainly had no recovery plan; but we set about brightening the corner where we were—literally. We put little electric candles or "friendship lights in each window fronting on the avenue. When you drove into town and rounded the curve that took you straight into Aliquippa, you could not help seeing those friendly flickering lights. They seemed to call out, "Be of good cheer. All is not lost." They were signs of hope, as were the flowers we grew in hitherto neglected front gardens of the row houses. Come springtime, the same drive down Franklin Avenue would expose a mass of colorful flowers blooming their hearts out. Here again hope was on display. Because we lived as a community and were more numerous than a typical nuclear family, the candles and the flowers made a greater impact. If nothing else, they surely made *us* feel better about living here. A sign of hope is what we were committed to being; and what we *all* needed to dispel the darkness of this place.

Celebration had daily Evening Prayer at 5:30 in the upstairs chapter—room of our office building. There were no curtains at the window, so passers-by on their way home from work could look up and see people praying there, if they allowed their eyes to wander in that direction. These things—a praying presence, signs of warmth and beauty provided by the candles and flowers—*these* constituted our first offering to the town of Aliquippa.

It could be seriously cold in the wintertime—the kind of cold that makes the hairs in your nostrils freeze up. Graham and I lived in the first row house, just where the road curves and a stoplight awaits. The frequent sound of eighteen-wheelers gearing down just twenty feet from the bedroom window was not conducive to good sleeping. Eventually we bought a noise-machine for Graham, who was a much lighter sleeper than I. Right across the street was a bar, a meeting-place for lots of nefarious exchanges. Despite its reputation as a violent place, Aliquippa had little actual street violence; domestic violence was another matter.

The good news was that we could look forward to being members of All Saints Episcopal Church, just a block away on Franklin Avenue. We could attend services, give our tithe, and get about the business of settling into our stateside life and traveling ministry. What a short-lived dream *that* turned out to be. We knew that the rector, The Rev. Chris Leighton, had set in motion a plan to spread the Episcopal Church's mission to Hopewell, a nearby affluent neighborhood, by taking half the congregation to provide leadership there while the other half remained downtown. It would be an intentionally divided parish, with two locations. He had shared this vision with Graham and Bill, so it was no surprise, although it may have seemed a bit curious.

The real surprise came in August, just a month after most of the community members from Scotland had arrived, when Chris announced from the pulpit that he was accepting a call to become rector of yet *another* church in the diocese. He was leaving for "greener pastures"—my words, not his. I'm sure that somewhere in the back of his mind was the consoling thought that no matter what happened, things would be OK now that Celebration was in town. Before we knew what had hit us, we were being left by default with a semi-abandoned church on our hands. It happened in stages, of course. But eventually—and who could really be surprised—this divided parish idea proved unworkable. Far fewer than half of the parishioners had hung in with the downtown location, and the larger Hopewell "half" was busy making sense of growing the church in their new and very nice neighborhood. They wished us well, I'm sure.

At this point All Saints, Aliquippa, was reduced to mission status in the diocese and Graham was asked to become its Vicar. Once before in his ministry back in Houston Graham had helped resurrect a dying church in the inner city. But this was different, for a lot of reasons. It was not going to happen here. Not that way; not this time. The Community of Celebration already had its plate full of ministry commitments. Picking up the pieces of an institutional church whose congregation had abandoned ship was not one of them. Yet the pieces were strewn all about us. Celebration had every intention of becoming productive citizens of Aliquippa, and responding to needs we felt we could meet.

But taking over a parish ministry was the *last* thing we had come here to do.

As we struggled with this dilemma new doors began to open. NBC featured our presence in Aliquippa on a Christmas program showing how God was still at work, still in the business of spreading joy where there had been gloom, still manifesting hope. As I sat back and viewed the 3-5 minute film I was amazed. I saw, juxtaposed, the wretchedness of Aliquippa and the blessedness of God's intent, God's passion for these people. I heard the beauty of the music, the voices of our children, blended with the lighted tree in the midst of this blighted town—*truly* an icon of hope. And I sensed the *mystery* of God the Spirit here at work in this place.

One day I stood at our kitchen sink washing dishes when my eyes were drawn to the hillside behind the rowhouses. High on that hill was a small band of folk sitting around a tiny campfire. It was misty outside, and I blinked my eyes so I could see them better. They seemed to be gazing at the avenue below, their eyes encompassing the town laid out before them. Their demeanor was one of compassion. I marveled at the sight. Then, I blinked my eyes once more: they were gone. As quickly as they had materialized they vanished. I had seen a vision: I had seen Jesus and his disciples gazing on the multitudes with compassion. And I knew our little motley crew was the small band 'camped out' on this hillside, sent here to *be* the compassionate presence of Jesus.

There was more ahead. There were protest songs when we marched in solidarity with the steel workers whose pensions had been denied. There were new songs and hymns emerging and somehow reflecting the soul-quality of this town. My own "protest hymn" of sorts was "Lord, who throughout these forty days," a jazzy setting of a traditionally somber hymn for Lent. For most African-Americans in our town—and they *were* in the majority—the sounds of a typical Protestant church organ were sepulchral. They seemed to beg the question, "So, where's the funeral?" I wanted my music to show the good news of Lent: that it's a time we can draw close to God, not be repelled because of our sinfulness.

Yet another Christmas event proved to be an eye-opener for me personally. I was asked to be co-director of an ecumenical service. The other director was from Church in the Round, the large *Church of God In Christ* congregation. We invited all the choirs in town to participate. Those who rallied to the call were St. Titus Roman Catholic Church, Church in the Round, and our folk from Celebration /All Saints. On the first night of rehearsal the Roman Catholics were asking, "So, where is the music?" I was circulating the printed songs as they spoke. The African-American folk from Church in the Round were asking, "So, where's the music? Sing us the tune." I realized they could have cared less about what was on a piece paper being passed around. For them, the music was *in the air* . . . Sing it, please. Being all things to all people took on new meaning for me that Christmas. Once again, music seemed to unite where *systems* failed; people from radically different backgrounds could sing the same song together—to the glory of God.

Again NBC showed up to film this ecumenical event. They asked Edith Washington, a prominent leader in a local African-American church, to comment on the poverty and sad state of Aliquippa. "Oh," she said, "we can't *think poor*. No, we can't even *think* poor . . ." Here she threw her head back and proclaimed . . ."because of what the LORD has done for us!" When she said that word *Lord* it rolled down the hillsides and through the Ohio River valleys, it rolled out across the countryside and brought hope to every trembling reed.

A brief digression: On a return visit to the States after some years in Britain, I was ruminating about the significance of *coming home*. I had not felt homesick while overseas, though I loved the places we had left. Somehow I managed to keep my eyes looking forward, not back, and that had worked for me. Yet there was a strange nostalgia about returning. What was it? We landed in New York, and I found myself straining to see the first stateside face. There he came: an airline employee rolling a wheel-chair onto the plane to collect a passenger needing assistance. The man's face was radiant; his smile covered all of it, and his teeth shone brilliant and white against his jet-black skin. "Aha. *That's* what I have missed." Suddenly it was crystal-clear to me: I had missed that infectious soul-quality which African-Americans have. My experience in the UK had been too white. It lacked something; this was it—which brings me to Horace.

Dr. Clarence Horace Boyer was a distinguished ethnomusicologist with whom I had served on the Episcopal Church's Music Commission. Getting to know Horace was one of the highlights of that experience. He had the aforementioned soul-quality—*in spades*. He was a highly educated man, but faithful to his ethnic roots; in fact, they had become the center of his research and expertise. He became renowned for a lecture-concert called "The Old Ship of Zion" in which he chronicled the history of the black community in America through its music. He was scheduled to perform this for us on Friday evening, February 10, 1990. Then on Saturday he would lead our choir in a workshop singing *black gospel* music. We were so excited. Flyers had gone out to area churches inviting them to the Friday night event, and a good number filled the church that evening. To our shock and dismay, we received a phone call from Horace saying he had been bumped off his flight from Boston, and could not get in until much later that evening. Panic stations.

Suddenly, we remembered. *This* was the night the whole world was on tiptoe, waiting, yearning, praying for Nelson Mandela's release after twenty-seven years of imprisonment on Robin Island, R.S.A. Still vivid was my memory of having stood on the tip of the Cape of Good Hope in 1982, gazing across the sea to that island of exile where many prisoners including Mandela were incarcerated. Now it seemed obvious what we needed to do:

Rounding up the Fisherfolk who had been in South Africa, we sang the songs we had learned there, celebrating the life of a yearning people. That evening focused around prayer for Mandela, their heroic leader, and his release. The void of Horace's absence was filled as we joined in an international, inter-racial, ecumenical prayer meeting that night. The rest is history. The great deliverance happened. Mandela *was* released from prison.

And—due in part to Dr. Boyer's delayed arrival—we had *been there,* participating in that historic moment in a very unexpected and exciting way. Thank you, Horace.

At this point in time I had almost completed the Freedom Mass which my sojourn in South Africa had inspired. I still needed a tune for *Pascha Nostrum,* or *Christ our Passover,* the bit that is sung at the breaking of the bread. Suddenly, I knew the tune to use. It came to me in a flash. It was the protest song the people of R.S.A. had sung during all those long years of Mandela's imprisonment. It was addressed to President Botha, and the words they used were these:

> *Open, Botha! we are a'knocking. Open, Botha! we are a'knocking.*
> *Release Mandela, our leader! Release Mandela, our leader!*
> From *Vula Botha,* R.S.A.

Mandela's release from prison was a sure sign to the people of R.S.A. that "Freedom is Coming"—just as Christ's bursting from death's dark prison to life eternal is a sign of new life for all who believe. So is it any wonder that the music fit the words of the liturgy?

Alleluia! Alleluia! Alleluia! Alleluia!

Christ our Passover is sacrificed for us. Therefore let us keep the feast.

We were in tune with the cosmos that weekend. We were participants in God's mighty activity here on earth. You could feel it; you could touch it. We had lived into a paradigm of God's redeeming work.

> *But the deliverance of the righteous comes from the Lord;*
> *he is their stronghold in time of trouble.*
> *The Lord will help them and rescue them;*
> *he will rescue them from the wicked and deliver them,*
> *because they seek refuge in him.*
> *Psalm 37: 41-42*

Twenty
Troubling Clouds

Life in Aliquippa continued into the early '90's, with Celebration's presence bearing varieties of fruit including a housing ministry—renting some of the row houses to local families needing a secure place and fair rental cost. The daily offices of Morning and Evening Prayer had become well-established time markers each weekday, bringing remarkable peace and order to the day's busy-ness. But there were troubling elements for me personally. It seemed difficult for me to break away from my musical role long enough to explore other ministries. Had I made myself indispensable to the music publishing part of our life? I had begun to feel like a music machine, and that wasn't good. I yearned to have more time just to be with people, to love and serve them in simple ways.

Graham was at an awkward place in his ministry also: trying to step back and allow others in leadership at Celebration to function freely, but almost needing another place to *be* in order for that to happen. We had talked about spending some time at Daphne Grimes' retreat center, *Thomas the Apostle,* in Wyoming; but we always ran into the problem of my being integral to the recording and publishing projects for Celebration. Graham had never had a sabbatical, and one would have been timely at this point. It was a complex situation for us.

There were also troubling incidents. One was when Graham's briefcase was stolen at a London airport, in the same week that our home, the Manse, was burgled and our household petty cash drawer raided. Both these incidents—happening close together in time—were unsettling to me, atypical of how well protected our life had felt until now. Not that I thought we *deserved* particular protection; but it had just always seemed to be there: as we were about the Lord's business, the Lord himself was watching over us and guarding us from harm. Now it felt like a hedge was being removed from around us. I began to experience brief periods of panic when I was in an enclosed space—like the shower. Why was all of this happening?

Fast forward to a recent morning quiet-time when the Epistle reading jarred loose a memory from 1992. From James 2: 12-13 I read: *So speak and so act as those who are to be judged by the law of liberty. For judgment will be without mercy to anyone who has shown no mercy; mercy triumphs over judgment.*

Mercy triumphs over judgment. Oh, really? Where? Where is that happening? Where is that so?

These words from James' Epistle jolted me back to one particularly painful day in my life. It was the summer of 1992, when Graham and I were headed to North Carolina to visit *the ladies,* Bey and Jane, my nonagenarian mother and aunt. Both of them were precious to both of us. The plan was to leave Aliquippa very early that morning for the long drive south. The car was all packed and ready to go—a nice Ford Taurus borrowed from companions of Celebration especially for this trip. But that morning something had come up that detained Graham on the phone for a while, so I puttered about until he was ready to leave. He seemed unusually quiet, somewhat tense, as we drove out and headed for the interstate. After a few minutes I said,

"Where are we going to stop for breakfast?"

"I don't know. Let's get down the road a bit . . ."

Finally we did stop at a Shoney's—the place with the big breakfast buffet and the big people eating it. I was hungry and put away my breakfast well enough, but Graham ate very little. I wondered what was wrong, but he brushed it off saying he just wasn't very hungry this morning.

Back down the road we drove . . . in silence. I knew something wasn't right. Finally we came to a place in the road wide enough to pull off and stop, and that is exactly what Graham did.

"We need to talk," he said. But it was he who did most of the talking. He told me about an accusation that had been made against him—dealing with sexual improprieties some years ago involving himself and a male member of the Fisherfolk traveling team. The accusations, made by the former team member's wife via her Episcopal Bishop, had been relayed to our bishop in Pittsburgh. And voilà!—without a day's delay, or time to talk to the bishop or any such humane provision, the news was out—in the papers, for heaven's sake. Graham had received a phone call from a journalist we knew, had told her something evasive and hung up the phone. Minutes later he called her back to say, "Yes, I am the man"—after the example of truth-telling ole' King David, I suppose, when he was confronted concerning Bathsheba. The journalist wasted no time getting to the Pittsburgh papers. I feel sure the bishop could and would have handled things more gracefully, given the opportunity. But the story was out.

I was stunned. I simply sat there in silence. I couldn't say a word for a long time. I knew that Graham had traveled to see several people over the past year—and this young man, living in London at the time, was one of them. Graham seemed to be on a personal mission of some kind. During the spring he had told me that he simply must find a spiritual director, someone outside the community who could be a sounding board for him. I thought that an excellent idea—without knowing anything more specific than that Graham seemed to be struggling inside himself, seemed to be trying to work some things out. I recalled the conference at Geneva College earlier that spring, when in our small break-out groups—we were in different ones—I had seen him weeping across the large hall from where I sat. So when he mentioned seeking a spiritual advisor I even made a suggestion or two about likely choices. In the end Graham chose a priest in New York, a man whom I had met on one occasion in Aliquippa. The priest had told him that his improprieties might be considered adulterous behavior in my view, and that he should share them with me.

And now . . . I seemed to be sharing them with the world. Surely I must have said *something* at some point, but for the life of me I don't know what it was, and I know I didn't have much to say. Just trying to absorb it all I was, and thinking *how quickly life can change right before your eyes.*

Graham was concerned of course about Bey and Jane and how we were going to handle things in Carolina. But he was keenly concerned about me—the silent partner in the seat beside him. He didn't try to pry words out of me; he knew I was in a kind of deep shock. I certainly was. But I was also putting together some pieces in my mind. Some things were beginning to make more sense than they had heretofore.

For years now I had taken comfort in our community lifestyle as a place where Graham could enjoy close relationships with other men—not to the exclusion of women, but a place where he could live into what I perceived to be his . . . bisexuality, I suppose. That word was not a part of my lexicon at the time. But I intuited the fact that Graham was a bigger-than-life sort of man who looked deeply into other souls and who needed a variety of friends around him who could benefit from that gift and could give back to him in some ways. I never once considered the sexual implications of my ruminations about all this. So, that was the missing piece of the puzzle that was beginning to fit together.

On we drove, through the beautiful mountain stretches of West Virginia, through several summer storms, and on into the Carolinas. Our usual warm southern welcome awaited us. Those intrepid women, Bey and Jane, were there to hug us and "bless our hearts" and receive us with open hearts. These were the same women whose prayers and support had helped sustain us through years of ministry overseas. Bless *their* hearts. The bonds of love were strong between us.

Half an hour after our arrival a phone call came for Graham. He was on the phone briefly, then summoned me. "The bishop wants to speak to you, Betty," he said. I went into the library of the old home place where one could have a private conversation. The bishop got right to the point:

"Betty," he said, "This must surely have been the most awful day in your entire life." I remember pausing before I answered, then saying, "Well, yes . . . *and* no."

"Oh, it *has* to have been," he summarily concluded. Our conversation was not lengthy, but I do recall telling him, "I am praying for God's mercy for all those involved."

And, I most surely recall his answer to that: "Oh, no. We need to know the whole truth. It's the *truth* that matters here."

I was stunned by his answer. *You mean, my dear bishop, that God's mercies do indeed fail? You mean there are situations where mercy is meaningless? Mercy and truth have not met together? Just what do you mean?*

Clearly, there were no answers forthcoming.

It was a different sort of vacation than either of us had anticipated. On the day after we arrived we drew together not only Bey and Jane, but also my brother and a dear friend in Burlington. We sat down in the den while Graham explained the situation to them in simple, direct terms. He handled it so well, so truthfully. He made no excuses. He asked their forgiveness. We also went to see another Burlington couple who had been friends for forty years. He did the same with them. I said very little, but I prayed a lot. Both these confessionals went extremely well. They required enormous courage on Graham's part; they required enormous love and forbearance on the part of this close circle of friends and relations. But clearly, the direct way was the best way. The very best way. And clearly, the bonds of friendship were deep and strong in this place.

Our own children were, of course, not able to be present. Graham spoke to them by phone—a second-best way but the only way available at the moment. He told them we would be coming to Texas soon, and wanted to be able to sit down with them as well. That covered four of the six. He was able to spend time with our Carolina son, leaving only our Vancouver daughter "uncovered"—as her husband refused to allow her to speak to Graham on the phone. That was deeply painful.

To say that the news cast a pall over our vacation would be right. We did our best to *be* our best for one another. Bey and Jane were past masters at putting the best spin on things, at being positive and not negative. Because I knew them so well, maybe I was the only one who noticed a slight drooping of the shoulders, as if they were carrying a heavy load. They were. We all knew it. Our life seemed to have gone suddenly under a cloud. Graham scanned the local papers to see if any publicity had made it this far south of Pittsburgh. We saw nothing, but several times when we took morning walks Graham noticed a car following at some distance, and wondered if some industrious reporter was scouting around. Being under surveillance—which is how it felt—was uncomfortable. We started walking less, and stayed home at Bey's more. Even here there was unease. Graham wanted more than anything to spare the ladies every discomfort that could be avoided.

What were we going to do next? That was the question. The first answer came in a directive from our bishop for Graham to go to Tampa, Florida for several days of psychiatric evaluation and consultation. I saw him off on the train and waited. The waiting seemed interminable. Our life—as we had known it—was hanging in the balance, altogether out of our control. We were staring into an unknown future. Graham, of course, had a schedule to keep in Florida, things to do, appointments to keep, but he must have felt some of the same anxious feelings that were visiting me. At one point I remember picking up the phone and calling my dear friend Cattie, who had been with us at Graham's confessional a few days earlier. I said, "Please pray for me. I am having some kind of panic attack. I feel like I'm about to jump out of my skin. I feel so anxious." It was true: *Henny, Penny, the sky is falling in* was my mood of the moment. I knew she would pray, and talking to her helped.

Over the next week, Graham returned from Tampa and we made our way back to Aliquippa—a torturous home-coming, but unavoidable under the circumstances. Many details have faded mercifully from my memory; leaving the bare agony of feeling *estranged,* separated from our friends by this thundercloud that had overcast all of our lives. The *Manse* which had been our home for four years sat on a hill overlooking Franklin Avenue. It now seemed like an island surrounded by a moat, isolated from the mainland which was our community. From time to time a Celebration member would climb the hill just to check in on us, but there was no occasion to be with or share with the whole community. They, like we, were in a state of shock, and uncertain of the way ahead for us all. Additionally, they were undoubtedly anxious about possible legal action which might affect them. We inquired about coming to All Saints for the Sunday Eucharist, and were advised that it was probably unwise. Graham commented ruefully, "Well, it's not the first time I have been ex-communicated." He was recalling his youthful experience in the Roman Catholic church, when he *was* quite literally ex-communicated.

Our youngest daughter Martha flew up from Texas just to be with us and help in any way she could. On August 11, 1992, she walked down the hill with me and held my hand on the way to the fateful meeting with the bishop—fateful because our future was in his hands. Graham had gone down earlier at the Bishop's request; now it was time for me to join him at a meeting which included the two of us, the Bishop and the head of the Standing Committee from the Diocese, plus the two Guardians of Celebration. All I remember clearly from that meeting was the sight of Bill Farra, one of the two Guardians, sitting there quietly weeping the entire time. He has since told me it was the hardest day of his life. It was certainly one of the hardest in mine. And I cannot fathom how Graham must have been feeling.

The results of this meeting were two-fold for us: Our membership in the Community of Celebration was suspended, and Graham's priestly ministry was officially inhibited by the

Bishop "until such time as these allegations"—of sexual abuse—"are properly resolved." So now at least we knew where we stood. We had become exiles; now we had to live into that reality. We would be going to Texas, living for a time with our daughter Martha and her husband, while both of us received counseling from a therapist who had been recommended by the Florida evaluation team.

Now all we had to do was pack up and go. No farewell parties, nothing like that. Just . . . pack up and go. Ah, but there was one All Saints parishioner who asked us to come for a bite of supper on the night before we planned to leave. That was so kind of them, and *felt* like a farewell party. There were a few details that needed tending to before we left. I went to a local jeweler's to pick up my wedding band which had been there for sizing. While in the store I could hear whispers behind my back, and a snide comment . . ."Some marriage, eh?" Clearly the publicity had had its effect in the local community. Then there was the road trip to Ann Arbor, Michigan, to see Graham's dentist of many years, Harry McIntosh. We had turned in our Celebration credit card which we customarily used on road trips for gasoline, etc. We had to scramble to find enough cash for gas; we were just unaccustomed to this new way of living *sans community*.

Sometime during the journey Martha noticed it was September 1, Graham's and my 41st anniversary. "So . . ." Martha queried from the back seat, "Where are we going to have the anniversary *dinner*?" We tossed that about for awhile, and in the end did the only thing that was obvious and practicable: we went to a McDonald's! It was on our route back to Pennsylvania. We enjoyed every mouthful; this was a unique way to celebrate an anniversary—especially remembering the gourmet feasts which Graham himself had often prepared. This was like comic relief, and we needed a good laugh.

Life in Texas was different; but we were there for a purpose and set about addressing it. Martha and her husband Lee had invited us to stay with them in their tiny, less than 1000 square feet, rental home. They prepared for our arrival by moving out of the master bedroom and giving *us* the king-size bed, while they slept in another room on the floor. They could not have been kinder; they were offering all they had in a situation which they knew was difficult for us. We were humbled by that. It was by all accounts a very small home: Lee once remarked that you had to go outside even to change your *mind*. Never mind your underwear, or whatever else might need changing.

Of course, the rhythm and pacing of our life changed. Graham and I continued reading the Morning Office together. Graham took delight in walking Martha's dog *Polo*, and it was real therapy for me to drive over to Mary and John's and practice on their piano. On occasion we explored additional sources of income, as we were limited at this point to Graham's Social Security plus $500 per month from Redeemer friends who took turns supplementing our income. We applied for a job managing a storage unit, but were turned down as "over-qualified." Maybe they didn't think we'd be strong enough to deal with the physical demands of the job. Graham applied at McDonald's, who were hiring quite a few retirees. I recall how this hit me in my gut: that this man of such extraordinary gifts was applying for work in a fast-food chain. But Graham never thought a thing about it. He did what seemed practicable, what was realistic at the time.

We went weekly to our respective appointments with the therapist, and they were helpful. He happened to be on staff at a local Lutheran church and invited us to attend, since a church home was clearly one of the missing ingredients in our life. We worshipped there every Sunday for some months, and were happy to be included and warmly received. We also attended a weekly twelve-step meeting at the invitation of Keith Miller who had reached out to us from the time he knew we were in Austin. The group he had started was called "Sinners Anonymous" and was comprised of people from a variety of addictive backgrounds. *Sin,* according to Keith, was the *real* addiction, the universal addiction. So we could all find a place around that table.

Another gift of God's mercy came through a retired bishop, Bishop Cox, who arranged to meet us at a local Episcopal church to hear Graham's Confession, and to celebrate Eucharist with us. His wife was present also. Then, sometime in February we were contacted by a young woman we had known at Redeemer, Houston, who invited us to the Ash Wednesday service at St. Matthew's, Austin. It was the first overture of a personal nature from an Episcopal lay-person other than Keith, and we planned to attend.

Before Ash Wednesday rolled around, however, Graham began to have heart symptoms, something to do with the rhythm of his heart. He entered the hospital on Ash Wednesday to undergo tests, and we never had opportunity to respond to that kind invitation from a well-intended Episcopal lay-woman. However, every slight move in our direction was appreciated times many.

How great is your goodness, O Lord!
which you have laid up for those who fear you;
which you have done in the sight of all
for those who put their trust in you.
You hide them in the covert of your presence from
those who slander them;
you keep them in your shelter from the strife of tongues.
Blessed be the Lord!
for he has shown me the wonders of his love in a besieged city.
Psalm 31: 19-21

Twenty-one
Going Home

How many times had we driven from Texas to North Carolina over the years? Many times. This time was different. From the start there was a purpose-driven quality about it. A phone call from Bey barely caught us as we were leaving Austin, telling us Aunt Jane had fallen and broken her hip that afternoon. All their well-intended neighbors—the ones who said "Call me if you need anything"—were not at home that afternoon. After Bey's struggle to get help, Jane was safely in the hospital now, receiving care. Bey's call urged us to come as quickly as we could manage.

We had planned to spend the night in northeast Texas with our old friends Bob and Nancy Eckert. However, with this latest news, we paused only long enough to have supper with them, then hastened on. Graham stayed at the wheel the entire time. I offered to relieve him but he wanted to drive. He almost seemed *driven* to drive. We stopped late that night at a nicer-than-usual motel; I remember demurring a bit over the cost, but Graham smiled and said, "This is our time away! Let's enjoy it." I always seemed to be the penny-pincher in the crowd. The same was true when we stopped for dinner the following evening: usually we didn't eat this high-off-the-hog these days, but Graham seemed in a semi-celebratory mood. Maybe it was just getting away from Austin, the tight accommodations, the prescribed activities. Or maybe it was a precursor of things to come . . .

Alamance County Hospital was a familiar sight in Burlington. It was there that our eldest son Bill was born in 1953, there that my father died in 1970. Now here we were visiting Aunt Jane and hearing about the accident that had caused her fall. Our turning up was a great relief to Bey. We could chauffeur her to and from the hospital while Jane was out of commission. One day I drove Graham there because he was once again having those fluttering sensations in his heart. While waiting on the doctor, Graham turned to me from the examining table, smiled and said,

"I think you need to turn me in for a new model."

"I'm not *remotely* interested in finding a new model," I said firmly. He was examined and released.

By the last week of March Aunt Jane was discharged from the hospital and came home, with a physical therapist assigned to make home-visits in the weeks ahead. She was a familiar friend to Bey and Jane, a member of their church. Jane, for her part, was a real trooper when it came to grasping the nettle and *just doing it*—despite the obvious discomfort. On April 1 the therapist came in the early afternoon for a session with Jane. This seemed the perfect moment for us to dash out and do the grocery shopping, one of the things that was proving helpful to Bey.

"Let's go to Winn-Dixie," Graham said. "They have a sale on salmon; the ladies need their heart food."

Grocery list in hand, we drove there, dividing up the list and beginning to comb the aisles for what we needed. Cereals were on my list, and I had already placed several in the cart when suddenly shots rang out in the store. It was an unmistakable sound; these were no firecrackers. I began to look in adjacent aisles for Graham, but didn't see him. But a male voice rang out from the front of the store:

"Everybody to the back of the store. *Get down! Down!*"

In a moment I spied Graham, near the back of the store but heading to the front.

"What's the trouble?" he frowned, clearly setting out in the direction the shots had come from.

"They're telling us to go to the back of the store," I said. *"Come on, let's go."*

Hesitating for a moment, he followed me. It was against his nature *not* to go where the trouble was. We walked past the meat counter into the butcher's domain where it was freezing cold. The butcher was just now absorbing the fact that there was a gunman loose in the store. I glanced down at the large lethal knives lying on the wooden chop-blocks and had the fleeting thought that at least the butcher had his own weapons handy. About that time Graham said, "I've got to sit down somewhere."

There was no place to sit there, so we stepped through swinging doors to the back passage-way hoping to find something. No seats there either. I said, "Lean on this . . ."—though I have forgotten what that *this* was. He leaned on it for a few seconds and the next thing I knew he collapsed at my feet.

"O God!" *What to do?* We were all alone in this passageway. I had not been trained in CPR, and here we were. Graham was lying on his back, not responding. I left him long enough to stick my head through the swinging doors and call for help. My cries sounded pale and thin, *sotto voce,* even though in my mind and heart I was screaming at the top of my lungs. Why was no one responding? I leaned over Graham and made some feeble attempt at mouth-to-mouth resuscitation but I was too weak to revive a field-mouse. *Where is everybody? Why is no one coming?*

I began to pray in tongues, the gift God gives us when cognitive languages fail and spirit calls out to spirit.

The minutes were ticking by. I went out once more, this time past the meat counter into the back aisle of the supermarket. I cried out for help once again. There was one young man there who heard me and came back to see what he could do. "There's mass confusion up there," he said, pointing to the front of the store. "Several people have been shot. I'm sure the ambulances will be here soon." I wish I knew that young man's name and could thank him just for wanting to help.

When the ambulance arrived almost fifteen minutes had gone by, and in my heart of hearts I knew that was too long. Too long for the brain to survive. However, as we drove to the hospital the EMS crew was able to resuscitate Graham, and he was admitted to Alamance Memorial Hospital. I phoned Cattie—thank God she was home—and asked her to go be with Bey and Jane, and tell them Graham had collapsed but was still alive . . . or something like that.

The next fifteen days were an indescribable mixture of sorrow, grief, and thankful recollection. Graham was in a coma, underwent various tests to determine the viability of the brain stem, and was lovingly tended by doctors and nursing staff. Meanwhile our children gathered from the four winds—from Texas, from Vancouver, B.C., from Colorado, where Nathan had been on a skiing holiday. My sister Nancy came from Texas also, and parked her guitar in the bathroom of Graham's assigned hospital room, since clearly *he* was not going to be using it. She would sing to him quiet songs of faith we had all known and loved. Bill Farra came down from Aliquippa to be and stay with us. Graham's two Canadian sisters came and joined in the vigil. Every night around eight o'clock we would gather around Graham's bed and say and sing *Compline,* that wonderful office designed to comfort us at day's end. At first we quietly closed the door to his room so as not to bother anyone else. But then the nursing staff asked us to leave it open, as many of the patients on the hall said they were blessed by the music and wanted to hear it better.

This was a blessed time—this singing and praying together at the end of the day. We were *singing him over* as the African-American community understands it. Gradually each of the children was living into the reality of losing their father in this earthly life. They were being invited to release him into the arms of a loving heavenly Father. From the very day of his cardiac arrest I knew in my spirit that this is the way it would be. But the coma was a gift from God. It provided us all, and especially the children, time to bridge that gap, to walk the walk with Graham, to touch him, to sing to him, to clip his beard or shave him (the boys were good at this), and pour out our love in whatever ways we could. On Palm Sunday my priest and pastor David Williams came to the hospital and celebrated Eucharist with our family group—following his busy morning of services at the church.

Then on Friday, April 16, Graham went home to heaven. Commenting on this particular day, a young woman from Pittsburgh for whom Graham had been a spiritual father, said, "I prayed that he might die on Good Friday. In the end he *did* die on the Orthodox Good Friday, a date which Orthodox Christians feel is reserved for the truly blessed." Bill Farra and I were with him when he passed away. We were singing "Rock of Ages." Moments after he breathed his last, a fire alarm went off in the building. It was short-lived, but Nathan reckoned it was the fire of Graham's spirit shooting up to heaven. He was there now; we were here. One thing was certain: our lives would never be the same for having known and loved him.

The weeks of bedside vigil were tranquil in comparison to planning the funeral. This was complex, with a lot of inner turmoil for me: unresolved feelings concerning our bishop, the Celebration community, the Episcopal Church and how it cared for one of its own clergy. In the end I took no steps to block any who might want to attend the funeral; neither did I go out of my way to include them. It was beyond my ken, and I needed time for some of these issues to find resolution—if indeed they ever did. One significant blessing was the arrival of the beautiful white funeral pall from Redeemer Church, Houston, for draping over the coffin during the service. Since it was Eastertide that seemed ever so appropriate, and preferable to the purple pall available at Holy Comforter.

Our beloved Margi, former daughter-in-law but daughter in the spirit forever, came from Long Island and offered her ministry of liturgical dance at the funeral. As we planned the service I remember telling David Williams how I would love for Margi to be able to share that gift during the liturgy. It was not the usual "done" thing in this traditional church, but then Graham was not your usual traditional person. He was among other things an inspired worship leader, not afraid to step out and try something different if the spirit urged him . . . David listened, he heard my heart, and I have always been grateful for his sensitivity to our needs at that time. In the service, Margi lent movement and grace to the singing of one of Graham's favorite hymns, *My Jesus, I Love Thee,* encircling the bier as she danced. It was beautiful and altogether appropriate. Our little family group sang a setting of Psalm 84 that hearkened back to our Fisherfolk troubadour ministry in Britain. And at the graveside committal service we sang our own Fisherfolk setting of the *Nunc Dimittis,* with guitars strumming sweetly in accompaniment.

Graham was the second male member of our family to be interred at Pine Hill Cemetery during Eastertide. The first was my father back in 1970. What a blessed time to die! And blessed for the family too, because they drew such comfort from the season itself, where we are constantly reminded in the daily lectionary and services of the church that "Christ *is risen. He is risen indeed! Alleluia!"* This assurance was invaluable as I made my step by step grief journey over the next months.

Surprisingly, one of the first big hurdles was simply *being* with Bey and Jane. Although I was grateful for their constant love and presence, I was also mindful of their fragility. For some reason—I guess it was post-traumatic stress—that's all I could think about now. How could I cope if they needed help? Here we were under the same roof, and now I was their security system. I had failed Graham in his hour of distress; so how could I be responsible for these two old ladies in a crisis? Cattie and I went away for a few days to her beach house, and we talked about this challenge. *Lifeline* to the rescue! This local ministry was available to those who felt vulnerable and needed someone to contact in an emergency. It was the perfect solution, and mind you, *I* was the one feeling vulnerable. It hadn't occurred to Bey and Jane that they were, because of course they had each other.

Another timely trip was one to Connecticut to see longtime friend Virginia. She had recently been widowed and stood ready, as always, to be my friend. I cried a lot while I was there with her. We had been to her church in Ridgefield and the rector acknowledged my presence and made a point of thanking me for the beautiful music I had brought into the Episcopal Church. When we got home to Virginia's, I remember screaming out through my tears of anguish, "What about *Graham?* Who is going to thank *him? He's* the one who needed the recognition." Well, many did thank him—in several memorial services, and also through the letters that poured in to me, acknowledging his unique contribution to the renewal movement of the sixties and seventies. I pray that through the spirit he has received those gifts in heaven.

As the dust began to settle a bit from these traumatic happenings, I couldn't help recalling Graham's words to me as we had driven from Bey and Jane's down to Texas in the late summer of 1992. He said: "When we are done with this assignment in Texas"—here he had reference to the required period of therapy—"I hope we can come back and stay with Bey and Jane to help them in their golden years." He was thinking, I have no doubt, of all the ways they had helped *us* over the years—as intercessors for our ministry, as financial supporters as they were able, and keeping their home fires burning so that our children had a stateside *anchor*, a place of love and belonging. More than any other influence, Graham's words helped me make a decision about what I was going to do next. Since he had wanted us to be here with Bey and Jane, and was no longer able to share that ministry, it was up to me now. I decided I would be that person and make that commitment on my own—feeling very sure of the Lord's sustaining help and Graham's intercessions. I have never *ever* regretted that decision.

So Graham went home to heaven. And I—for the present—went back to my birth home.

> *Happy are they who dwell in your house!*
> *they will always be praising you.*
> *Happy are the people whose strength is in you!*
> *whose hearts are set on the pilgrims' way.*
> *Psalm 84: 3-4*

Twenty-two
Life With Bey And Jane

There was plenty of room for me at Bey and Jane's, my family's home since I was eight years old. There was room for me then; there was room for me now. At this point I was—what shall I say—homeless? In a sense I was. Here I even had a special room I could call my own; it was the library, which had been my Daddy's hangout. Bey and Jane now lived essentially in the back of the house, opening up the living-room and adjacent library only when company came, after the manner of the old-timey parlor. The piano was there. I could play the piano, and I could use my newly acquired Smith-Corona word-processor. I set it on top of Daddy's big old desk. Funny thing that: before we had left Austin on our trek to Carolina, Graham had said to me:

"Aren't you going to take your new toy?" He was referring to this glorified typewriter with some memory.

"I hadn't planned to," I said.

"I think you'd enjoy having it," was his response. So I put it in the back seat of the car. Now as I reflect back, he must have been thinking ahead in some mystical way. He must have known deep inside that we were not going back to Texas. Maybe that is why he seemed so driven to drive the whole distance from Texas to Carolina, like someone who sites a goal and heads for it.

Over the next months I used the word-processor a lot. I wrote business letters on it, trying to get a sense of where on earth I was in this new set-adrift state. There were medical bills and funeral expenses to pay for Graham; there was correspondence concerning my ongoing financial resources now that I was no longer part of the Community of Celebration's regular financial structure. Nor did I want to be a burden to them, bearing in mind one of Graham's desires: that the small band of folk in Aliquippa not be weighed down by having to care for us in our "retirement." People were very kind on all fronts, and my needs were met in a variety of ways.

There always seemed to be lots to do. Some of it revolved around helping Bey and Jane. I became Aunt Jane's steady chauffeur, driving her to her medical appointments. Her favorite expression while easing herself into the passenger seat was: "Just wait 'til I get my hind foot in." She was remarkable, in that she had had several chronic medical problems dating from her twenties when she was hospitalized with an appendectomy and ended up with phlebitis. The remarkable part was her failure to mope about and complain. She also had terrible feet—a congenital problem which meant painful walking, for one thing. Aunt Jane stayed cheerful in spite of it all. She loved to talk to things: she talked to people if they were around, and if not she talked to creatures outside, to the stubborn drawer that wouldn't open easily, to the over-sized tomato she was trying to cram into a canning jar: "Just get *in there.*"

Bey was the leader of the duo. She called the shots, make no mistake. And Jane was a faithful follower. As the saying goes, it takes two to tango, and they had a beautiful dance of life going on. It all started back in 1970 when my daddy died. The memory of his funeral thrills me to this day, as I recall the thunderous sound of male voices. A majority of the practicing lawyers in North Carolina had turned up, raising the roof of the Methodist Church with *All Hail the Power of Jesus' Name.* A few nights before, on the day he passed away, my Aunt Jane had come over from her house a half-block away. She came over to spend that night with Bey, and never went home again. My dad used to chuckle and say about them, "When one of them is hurt, the other one bleeds." So, there you had it.

They had always been close friends. Not all sisters experience this, but they did. From their teen years when they pulled on jeans and boots and old shirts and romped through the brambles picking blackberries, and canned prize-winning tomatoes, winning the 4-H award for their county, they had been close companions. They were there for each other—always. Bey set the pace; Jane followed. On auto trips, even just around town, Bey said where they were going and Jane drove them there. They ran a great kitchen together, Bey doing the primary cooking, Jane specializing in the baking and the clean-ups after meals. Their canning career lasted for *eighty five years*. Jane's specialty was pear honey, a family favorite. I recently used up my second quart of tomatoes canned in the year 2000, when Bey was 101.

Their remarkable kitchen career was sustained by a garden which Bey and her helper James Woods maintained. James had worked for our family since the 1940's, and knew how things grew, when to plant and prune, and how to feed and water living things. Bey was the architect of the garden, and James had the hoe in hand. "If I were a rich woman," I often thought as I hummed *Fiddler on the Roof's* tune, I would hire a portrait-painter. I would have the artist paint Bey and James working together—she on her little wooden chair pointing to the very spot where the pansy needed to be planted, James right beside her with the tools to get the job done. How many times have I gazed in wonder at that scene. I even took photos, just in case that portrait painter ever showed up, or my *ship came in*.

Friends and neighbors could see the garden as they passed by on the street, and knew the ladies loved to "put up" vegetables and fruits in the summer. So with increasing frequency garden-fresh produce would appear on the back stoop, a gift from some neighbor who had an over-supply or lacked time to deal with it. The cardinal rule of this house seemed to be "On the back steps by morning; into a jar by nightfall." This was their version of the proverbial *waste not, want not*. They were serious about it. Sometimes I was tempted to find a spare octagonal "Stop!" sign and put it at the bottom of the back stairs. *Enough is enough* was my mantra, because the labor involved was quite taxing and poor Jane's arthritic hands were put to the test by all that peeling and preparing. They need a break sometimes, I thought to myself. Their neighbors are killing them with kindness.

Most of the time, though, I did little to interfere with their established routines and behaviors. After all, this is what had kept them going for over ninety years. Who was I to change things around? Instead, I tried to watch and learn from them. Over the Sunday dinner table they loved to hash over the service they had just attended. Sometimes it was funny:

"Jane, that was a splendid sermon this morning, don't you think?"

"Betty, now you know I can't hear *half* of what's said in church." Then after a minute she continued, "Did you see the Mayos down near the front? They're home from their trip."

"For heaven's sake, Jane. You know I can't see three feet ahead of myself, so how could I possibly see *them?*"

Life was never dull with Bey and Jane. They could be very playful, as when they introduced themselves to strangers by saying, "We had the same mother and father, but we are *not* sisters!" When that left people looking puzzled, they hastened to explain, "You see, our grandmother was a *man*, and our grandfather was *not!*" With eyes dancing merrily, they would let the strangers grapple with the conundrum, finally having mercy on them and giving them some hints:

They were *Knott* sisters, as a matter of fact.

Their grandmother's maiden name was *Mann*.

Their grandfather was Fielding *Knott*.

Years ago their love of reading had borne fruit for the entire church family at First Baptist when Bey started a church library. As always, she was the up-front leader, and Jane was her right-arm support person. Using her lifelong skills as a fourth-grade teacher, Jane took charge of all the library graphics, ran reading contests for young people in the summer, and kept an attractive display board outside the library itself. At one point a dozen lay-workers were involved in the library ministry. Bey herself had a prodigious memory and could "pull down"—as she liked to say—hundreds of poems, Shakespearean speeches, Biblical passages, from her memory's treasure trove. This was a comfort to her as her blindness increased. She could *still* pull down and enjoy those things committed to memory. She and Jane together had a collection of little verses and proverbs that could keep you smiling on a rainy day:

> *We's all constructed differently,*
> *No two of us the same;*
> *If we're good, we can't take credit,*
> *If we're bad, we ain't to blame!*

Bey and Jane were a good tonic for me, and a wonderful example of how to grow old without *really* growing old at all. Their playful child was always there, ready for a romp. And when things got rough, they were steady as a steel beam. In August, less than four months after Graham's unexpected departure, I began to have heart symptoms one evening after supper. Graham had always asked, if I complained of any chest discomfort, "Are you perspiring? Do you feel clammy? Do you feel nauseated?" This time the answers were uniform: *Yes. Yes. Yes!*

Bey called 911 for me, and I lay down on the floor, having earlier taken an anti acid medicine to no effect. The ambulance arrived, and off I went to nearby Memorial Hospital, the very same hospital where Graham had been taken in April. Even the doctor on call was the same. Believe me, he looked a bit pale when he recognized the name. After a few minutes of examination a helicopter from Duke Hospital was on its way. As I was airlifted off the pad I looked down and saw Bey waving to me from below. My little ninety-three-year-old mother had called 911, seen me off to the hospital, and was waving me on to where more help was available, all the while praying her heart out. She was indomitable.

A week earlier, as I had strolled the sandy beach at Wrightsville where I was visiting Cattie, neither of us had the faintest idea what was waiting up ahead for me—open heart surgery, a six-way bypass. When Bey called Cattie to tell her I was in the hospital and explain the prognosis and plan, first she said, "You need to sit down while I tell you this. You're not going to believe it."

The surgery went well. My two youngest, Martha and David, had driven non-stop from Texas to get there beforehand, my sister Nancy was there, and brother Jim and wife Joyce as well. Cattie was there too, so I was well attended in person and in prayer. As I was wheeled in before surgery I felt a strong sense of the Lord's presence and had two distinct thoughts: that I was going to survive this, and that I was in some inexplicable way sharing Graham's broken heart. For there was little doubt that his heart had been broken by all that had transpired. All the king's horses and all the king's men couldn't put it back together again—not in this life. Joyce had her own perception concerning me. She said, "In the old days they would have said, 'She died of a broken heart.'" They probably would have, save for the life-saving medical intervention I received.

The day of my release from Duke Hospital was the longest day in history. It was Saturday, when things creep along at a snail's pace and everything takes longer. I had been in the hospital only five days, and can't honestly say I felt ready to go. But my young surgeon, who could have been mistaken for a high-school student, so youthful was his appearance, *said* I was ready to go. First, seventy staples had to be removed from my body. No problem—at least for the ones who did the removing. Also, I had been given a list of necessary medicines to get hold of before nightfall. The afternoon wore on and on. Will we get released and all the way to Burlington before the pharmacy closes? We wondered.

At one point David broke with protocol and brought a wheelchair from the main floor up the elevator to get me. He was apprehended by a nurse who explained he couldn't *do* that. But his pro-activity somehow got things moving faster, and we did make it back to get the prescriptions filled. Nancy drove me safely to Bey and Jane's as daylight faded. She parked outside the front of the house, where the steps were less arduous. First there was a long front walkway and I was already past exhaustion emotionally and physically. Bey and Jane were waiting with smiles and arms outstretched at the front door. They gave me courage to keep walking *somehow*—I'll never know how. Walking across the front porch, past the doorway, through the living room, down the long, long hallway to the very back bedroom of the house: this was my ultimate challenge. When I finally reached a bed to lie down on, I lay down. *Thank you, Lord.*

If getting here had been a challenge, getting to sleep was even more so. Every time I began to relax and doze off, I would suddenly *startle* myself awake. My body seemed to be saying, "The last time you went sound asleep, they cut me open and did terrible things to me. So *I'm not taking any chances on letting down my guard.*" Nancy became my sleep-angel, the one who guarded my bed, lay beside me so she could reach out and touch me when I was restless or ill at ease. Her nearness and comfort brought me peace.

Over the next weeks my three precious girls, Mary, Jane and Martha took turns being my home nurse. When the Psalmist spoke of the blessing of a quiver full of children (Psalm 126) he said a mouthful. I felt the heavens had opened and poured forth blessing into my life through my wonderful daughters. Friends also came to encourage me, among them Roger Gant, husband of my schoolgirl buddy Rose Anne. Roger had been through heart surgery earlier, and was able to cheer me on in recovery, and encourage me to get into cardio rehab—as Roger himself had done.

My grief work had unavoidably been put on hold because of heart surgery. To this day I regret the numerous sympathy letters and cards that went unacknowledged. By the time I got around to dealing with them, they were here and there, my focus had been perturbed, and somehow it never happened. I needed too much energy just to survive and adapt to my new life regimen: diet, exercise, etc. I also needed something else. Most people have a home to grieve in, a place full of memories of their loved one, where they can process all the panoply of feelings that happen in grief. We had no home when Graham died. So I became aware of needing to piece together some of the places we had lived, the places of meaning to us through the years. I needed this as part of my grief work.

In the spring of 1994 my son Nathan accompanied me to the U.K. to do just that. We visited Yeldall Manor in Berkshire, we trained to Scotland and spent time on the Isle of Cumbrae where we had lived for five meaningful years, we celebrated Easter with the small Celebration Community in Bletchingley in the south of England and trained in to London, having dinner at Graham's favorite Italian *bistro*. All of this was wonderfully helpful to me in contextualizing my grief. Place is important, I came to realize. And Nathan was a delightful companion in the way, always filled with good humor. Since I could seldom keep up with his walking pace, he was fond of looking back in my direction and saying, "Well, *c'mon then, my little ball n' chain."*

If my gait had slowed somewhat, the tempo of my life was surely doing that as well. Living with two nonagenarians—even the lively two God had given me—was a differently paced life. For the next ten years my primary ministry was *eldercare*. As expected, I felt strengthened and empowered by Graham's spirit, knowing that in some way known only to the Spirit of God, he was beside me, helping me from the heavenlies. After all, this was something we had purposed to tackle *together*.

Then there was the cloud of witnesses that gathered every Sunday at Church of the Holy Comforter. I'm not talking about just the ones you could see with your physical eyes; they were very important, but there was also this host of angels and archangels and all the company of heaven who joined in celebrating the Eucharist with us week by week. I was sustained by this heavenly food, this gathering of faithful ones to give God the honor due His name. The very name of my parish church was filled with meaning for me: holy comfort was what the Holt family had experienced when their 12-year-old daughter Emily died in 1911. As a thank-offering they gave the funds necessary for building this lovely neo-Gothic structure. They named it *Church of the Holy Comforter* as a testimony to the strength and comfort they had received during the time of their great loss. God's comfort, as they discovered and I was learning, is strong stuff. It is not squishy like sympathy. It is strong, like metal that has come through the refiner's fire. Such is the comfort brought by the Holy Spirit.

Though I walk through the valley of the shadow of death,
I shall fear no evil;
for you are with me;
your rod and your staff, they comfort me.
You spread a table before me in the presence of those who trouble me;
you have anointed my head with oil,
and my cup is running over.
Psalm 23: 4-5

Twenty-three
The Road Curves

We can never see what's around the next life-curve. Certainly there is no way I could have seen Herb. But there he was. There he just *was*. My friend Virginia thinks that Graham and Jesus got together and *sent* Herb. Perhaps they thought I needed help with Bey and Jane. Well, there was some truth in that as the two ladies marched on into their nineties. Jane was one of those whom social services refer to as the *frail elderly*. Bey, on the other hand, was elderly but adamantly un-frail. She was bold and vigorous as ever, but not exempt from little accidents that caused problems. Between the two of them I stayed busy—doing the shopping and increasing amounts of meal preparation, driving each of them to their medical appointments, keeping up with home helpers and paying them, and a zillion little domestic details. I commented one day to a friend that it was like running your own nursing home.

So here comes Herb Wendell. I had met him before—not just once but on several occasions. He had been a friend and benefactor of Celebration for years, clearly someone who was intrigued by the ministry and by a leader like Graham; a risk-taker knows a risk-taker when he sees one. Herb had helped organize the Fisherfolk's re-entry tour of 1984. And then in 1993 suddenly there he was at Graham's funeral. He was there; then he was gone—not staying around for the luncheon for out-of-town guests. This, I later found out, was typical behavior on his part. He knew where he wanted to be, and where he didn't: a pretty decisive fellow.

I didn't see him again until the year following my heart surgery. He phoned to see how I was recovering, and reminded me that *both* of us were now members of the "zipper club"—those who have undergone open heart surgery. Come to find out, he was now living just down the road thirty miles in Durham, where he had moved to be part of Duke Hospital's cardio-rehab program. He said he would like to drop by sometime on his way to Greensboro, where he went for meetings. I said OK, that would be fine; it would be good to see another survivor of the ordeal called by-pass surgery.

"The first time I came into your mother's house," he later told me, "I saw that baseball bat sitting in the corner." There was no baseball bat; he just made that up. What he saw was a woman scrutinizing him; she knew he was the one who had been calling and had even succeeded in making me *laugh* on the phone. She was—at the very least—curious. Pretty soon Herb had succeeded in charming the ladies into his fan club. He had all the right tools: flowers in season and out; greeting cards appropriately chosen; candy in colorful wrappers; balloons on special days: this guy knew how to spread good cheer where it was needed, and he had a generous heart. His own life had not been easy—far from it. He wanted to spend the rest of it being a blessing to others, but he did not want to be lime-lighted for it. In fact, I was startled when he showed me his fairly new business card, designed for retirement years. It read: *Herb Wendell / In Charge of Nothing / Responsible for Everything*

His auto license-plate went even further: *A.Nobody*, it said. He used to offer $5 to anyone who could tell him what the "*A.*" stood for. Few could, but the answer was "Anonymous." In his financial giving he was generous but wanted to remain anonymous. Bey took issue with him about calling himself a *nobody*, saying he was indeed a *somebody* in the Lord, and that was that. As I see it, Herb had spent so many years thrusting himself forward—as a promoter and salesman *extraordinaire*, as an up-front guy with a confrontational streak, a good trouble-shooter. Now he wanted to find a place of serving Jesus Christ that was totally removed from that push-and-shove world. Well, with two nonagenarians and a sixty-five year old heart patient I guess he had found a really low-key situation.

Herb began to come to Burlington more frequently, always bringing something that made the ladies smile, and sometimes taking me out to dinner, a nice respite from my nursing home-at-home duties. It was good to have someone to talk to who knew my background with Celebration, who had known Graham, and to whom I didn't have to do a lot of explaining. Also, being the father of seven children, he understood my concern for my own six and some of the struggles they were having. Also, Bey was right: he made me laugh. There hadn't been a whole lot to laugh about recently. Having a clown around was good tonic for me, and Herb was a clowning sort of guy.

As I got to know him better, I realized what a many-faceted gift we all were to one another. Herb brought good cheer to Bey and Jane; they in turn furnished a missing ingredient in his life. Herb had lost his mother when he was three and a half; he had never had a kindly aunt. He found *both* in Bey and Jane—the Lord seems to take delight in two-way streets. Our friendship blossomed along reciprocal lines as well. Herb had been divorced and had lived alone for fifteen years. I had been widowed for several years, and couldn't even *remember* a time I had lived alone. So there were similarities and stark differences too. We enjoyed each other's company. Nothing, however, could have prepared me for the revelation that came to me in the garage behind Bey and Jane's house.

Earlier, in February 1995, Herb and I had driven to Greensboro to attend a course for helping seniors ease into high technology. It answered questions like "what do you need a computer *for?*" It was about as basic as you could get, and that suited us just fine, as neither of us were real *techies*. One interesting thing however was that our first class fell on Valentine's Day. Somehow, as the day progressed, the two of us seemed to attract approving smiles and a few lifted eyebrows, especially from the waitress at our lunchtime restaurant. Had we become an *item?*

Back to the garage. One spring day when I went out to start Aunt Jane's car, that faithful old 70's Oldsmobile, I heard the Lord's voice as clearly as I ever have: *I want you to marry Herb Wendell.* I stood immobilized, stunned, right there in the garage with the car keys waiting obediently in my hand. *Marry him?!?* Oh, no, Lord." No such thought had entered my head until this moment, and I was quite sure—well, pretty sure—that none had entered his. We were good friends, that's all.

The impression would not go away. I remembered one occasion when I had made a day-trip to Durham to see Herb and his new roomer, Kevin Hackett from Celebration, now a student at Duke Divinity School. Herb had fixed up an efficiency apartment for Kevin on the ground floor of his house. Sometime that day I recall walking through the upstairs living-room and hearing with the ears of my spirit, "It is not good for man to live alone." I tucked it away in a corner of my mind without much examination. Certainly, any connection to me was totally missing. Still, the Lord seems to have been working on me at some emotional level, gliding right past my Myers-Briggs "T" function, my opinions about Herb like "he talks too much" or "he has some *really* strong opinions", and making me more appreciative of his buoyancy of spirit and chronic cheerfulness. One day when we had driven to Hillsborough for lunch at the historic Colonial Inn, I made a startling confession to Herb. I said, "I need to tell you something."

"What's that?" he asked.

"That you have somehow touched my womanhood." They were the words that came to me—to tell him that for me, the relationship had become sexualized, and that I was attracted to him. Then we went in to have lunch, and the rest is history. I guess, looking back, that I was the one who proposed—more or less. At least I paved the way for the topic to be addressed. Several issues had to be dealt with: for one, I said I had made a commitment to the Lord to be with my *ladies* 'til death did us part. *They* did not know that, but the Lord and I did. So I could not move away from Burlington, and needed to stay close to them. This would likely be a deal-breaker, I reckoned, because Herb had bought a lovely home in Durham just three years earlier. I, on the other hand, had no home of my own to offer.

"Not a problem," says Herb. "I will sell my home in Durham and we'll find a place near Bey and Jane, and I will *help* you carry out your commitment to them."

Second declaration: I wanted to keep my name, Graham's name, *Pulkingham*. It was our family name, the name of all my six children; it was also my professional publishing name.

"Not a problem," says Herb. His own children found it hard to believe that he had agreed to this, since he had never seemed very favorable towards women's lib.

Third declaration: I want to be buried in the Carr family grave-plot which my father purchased years ago with great intentionality. Leo put a lot of stock in family history, and I concurred with him that graves provide a good record of a family's footsteps in the sand.

Again, Herb was amenable; and there was even room for him in the same plot, I told him.

So it was that we were married on October 9, 1996 in the Chapel of St. Athanasius, on the grounds of Holy Comforter Church in Burlington. It was an extremely small wedding, with a handful of friends and one child to represent each of us—only it turned out to be two for me, as Martha was determined to be there if she had to crash the gate, which was of course unnecessary.

Herb and I found a modest home for sale on the same street as Bey's and less than three minutes away. *Perfect*. We moved in January 1997, allowing time for a few remodeling projects which adapted the house to our needs. Now we were able to drop in on *the ladies* regularly, as well as respond to unpredictable needs.

Every weekday morning we showed up for Morning Prayer with Bey and Jane and Savannah, their household helper.

Gathering in the den, a cozy room at the back of the house, one of us would lead the short service found on page 137 of the Book of Common Prayer, and Savannah would read the appointed Scripture lesson. Savannah had never learned to read as a child, but Bey's neighbor Alleine Cooper had *taught* her to read while she was in her employ. Now she was reading to us from the Holy Scriptures daily. Following the reading and a short reflection on it, usually from *Good News Daily*, we offered up to the Lord our thanksgivings and intercessions. That was a blessed half-hour near the beginning of the day which seemed to get us all headed in the right direction; it provided Herb and me an up-close look at how the ladies were doing, without being obvious about it.

Sharing meals, a vital part of any family's life, was certainly a part of ours. We always had Sunday dinner with Bey and Jane. Occasionally we took them out for a weekday lunch, usually at their favorite tea-room *Two for Tea*. And we enjoyed special feasts on birthdays, Christmas and Easter. When the inevitable calls came for quick action in emergencies, we were ready. I would speed over to Bey and Jane's; Herb would follow after securing our house. Then we would decide how to "divide and conquer." Oftimes that meant sending Herb with Bey to the emergency room while I stayed with Jane. However it worked there were two of us to cover the bases, praise God. There were periods when the emergencies seemed to multiply, and I would experience the "ambulance syndrome"—always expecting the phone to ring with a new and urgent need. My whole being felt on alert, waiting for the next call.

Aunt Jane was the first to leave on the heavenward journey. Following a broken shoulder and many weeks in a skilled nursing facility, she was able to come home again, released from a facility where few walked out on their own. She loved being back home, but clearly seemed on a downward trek. One day I will never forget: it took *three* of us—Herb, Savannah and I—to get Jane to the medical clinic for a routine appointment. She was rarely out of bed these days; the strength in her limbs had decreased severely. How we managed to get her into and out of the car I cannot possibly tell you. I just recall hearing the doctor say to me, out of Jane's hearing, "Don't bring her here again; I will come see *her.*" When we finally did get her back into her own bed, she sank down into it like she had just run a marathon; she had. Then something extraordinary happened. Herb drew up a chair beside Jane's bed; he reached out and held her hand, just sitting there quietly by her side for the longest time. No words were needed, no words were exchanged. His was a simple ministry of *presence*, of just being there with his friend Jane whom he loved, as she began her homeward journey.

Jane went home to God in June of 2000. Due to storm damages being repaired at First Baptist, her funeral service was conducted at my church, Holy Comforter. I have to laugh when I recall earlier conversations between Bey and Jane. They both loved the Episcopal liturgy, and Bey especially appreciated the centrality of the altar instead of the omnipresent pulpit in the Baptist church. When right-wing conservatives had virtually taken over the Southern Baptist Convention, the ladies were not amused. Bey had been the first woman deacon elected in her church *years* ago. Now women deacons were no longer being allowed by the powers that be, but Bey was quick to remind us that Baptists mostly do what they please in their own congregations. She was becoming exasperated with the reactionary trends in the SBC.

"I don't know *what* I'm going to do with these Baptists." she would say. "Sometimes I think I will just go across the street and get down on my knees in that nice Episcopal church."

Quick as a flash Jane answered, "*Yes.* And we can even use the same parking place." The churches sit adjacent to one another. Along about this time Bey started to refer to herself as an "Episco-baptist." So it seemed altogether right and proper that Jane's funeral took place in this worshipful space that they both loved.

****

Before another year had passed, Herb had followed Jane on the heavenward journey. One of the last things he said to me in Duke Hospital was this, "I want to die well. I learned that from Jane." Indeed he had, as he sat by her bed, as he observed her quiet piety, her calm acceptance of whatever the Lord deemed best. Hers was a godliness with contentment, something the Bible commends as signifying "great gain" for the Christian. So it was that Herb, the often rambunctious, frivolous, or confrontational one, faced his own death with grace and dignity. He was reading the morning lesson in his Bible when he had his fatal heart attack. He was reading from the fourth chapter of Philippians:

Do not be anxious about anything, but in everything, by prayer and petition, with thanksgiving, present your requests to God. The peace of God, which transcends all understanding, will guard your hearts and your minds in Christ Jesus. (vss.6 &7)

Herb was a special guy, and he deserved and got a special funeral. He had told me several times, "When I die, I don't want any moping around, any sad funeral. I like the street parades they have in New Orleans; they know how to celebrate." With the help of our parish musician, Charles Hogan, we gave Herb the closest thing we could find: musicians from the Alamance Jazz Band provided music before the service—pieces like *Just a Closer Walk with Thee*. At the very end they let loose with a rousing rendition of *When the Saints Go Marching In,* which had us all joining in the street parade. Herb's spirit was rejoicing, New Orleans-style.

In the months ahead, I ran across this little poem:

"God bless the soul with sunny heart who brightens up each day
By spreading seeds of cheerfulness while traveling on life's way.
God bless him for the stars of hope he sets in each one's sky;
For the encouragement he gives that causes folk to try . . . "
Beverly J. Anderson

When I first read these lines, my immediate thought was, "HERB." My mother, who knew and loved Herb well, had the same response. For this is precisely how the man lived his life: as though each day were a fresh challenge to brighten someone's path, lighten a heavy load, speak a word of encouragement, give someone a playful prod, or—at the very least, tell a funny story that would take your mind clean off your troubles and cause you to laugh. Herb was a great believer in the therapeutic value of laughter. As he often reminded me, he had spent too many years being too serious.

Now, mind you, he could be serious; he was by no means a Pollyanna sort of person. Gifted with a quick mind, he was capable of passionate involvement in issues he believed in and a steadfast devotion to people he loved. His ability to *read* people, to get to the heart of issues, to put together a plan of action for a cause—any and all of these could serve to keep him on an intense track, or "too serious" as he phrased it. So perhaps some of his cheerfulness was self-induced—a message to his own soul to *lighten up*. He always gave his mother credit for passing on happy genes. This was the mother who had died when he was only three-and-a-half, but whose smile, whose happy singing while rocking him in her lap, whose cheerful spirit coursed through his life without ceasing. All in all, Herb gets my prize for the most buoyant spirit, the most contagious optimism, the sunniest personality I have ever known. He would be the first to give God the glory for his ever-hopeful attitude.

"Out of your inmost being," Jesus promised, "will flow rivers of living water." This he spoke concerning the Spirit he would send. I think of Herb when I think of that generosity of spirit, that bubbling-up to meet all kinds of challenges and adversities, that unquenchable spirit of life which dwelt in him. God's image was clearly visible.

So here I am: a widow once more. This time I *do* have a place to contextualize my grief. It is our home, just two minutes from Bey's. Again the Holy Spirit touches my life through the sensitivity of our church musician. Our choir sings an anthem with words that speak directly to my heart:

> *When the house doth sigh and weep,*
> *And the world is drowned with sleep,*
> *Yet mine eyes the watch do keep,*
> *Sweet Spirit, comfort me, comfort me!*
>   Words by Robert Herrick

****

And then there was Bey. Dear Bey, who had never asked to be 100, who said *"It was God's idea, not mine,"* survived until she was 104. She did more than survive; she *lived* life fully, as fully as she could given certain limitations. She had been legally blind for years now, but you would never have guessed it when you came into her presence. She drank you in with her eyes, made you feel welcomed. You could be a bristling porcupine and she would find some soft spot in you to touch and encourage, to draw out. And somehow as she gazed at you, you would never know that you were a blur in her eyes. Instead, you would feel beautiful. You would know you were in the presence of one of God's great lovers.

During the last year of her life, Bey and I had two *ice-storm* adventures. The first was when we lost power in the midst of a frigid night. A chill ran down my spine when I awoke and heard crackling limbs outside. I reached for the light switch and nothing happened, and then the cold truth struck me: here I am in a big old house with no lights, no heat, and a 102-year old woman to keep from freezing to death. Once daylight came I contacted my pastor, David, and we tried various contacts that might turn up a generator. All the while I kept Bey in bed and covered up as best I could. David and Sarah, his wife, brought a great hot-soup lunch, and we continued our efforts to get heating help. By late afternoon David phoned to say, "Enough.

Get ready. We're coming to get you and Bey, and you will stay at our house." He drove his four-wheel-drive vehicle clear up to Bey's front steps, and with the able assistance of four men from the church—enough to have carried us out on stretchers, though that wasn't needed—we were safely tucked away in a warm vehicle and on our way to a warm house. We stayed there for three days, in the company of several other *refugees,* and ever afterwards my mother referred to my pastor affectionately as *"our* David." He really was.

The other ice storm had a hero named David too. My son and his music group, headed by *Alejandro Escovedo,* were on route from eastern Carolina to Asheville for a gig that very night. David had told them about his grandmother, and also about a great barbecue place in Burlington, and the combination worked. They phoned to say they were going to stop by briefly. *Alas.* An hour before they were due the power went off. We hastily built a fire in the library fireplace, bundled Bey into a wheel-chair with lots of blankets, and waited. No hot coffee would be available, regrettably. But, braving wind and tempest, here they came—all four of them—climbing the treacherous icy back steps, *carrying* their precious instruments into the house, where they unpacked them and took off their heavy boots. Meanwhile David hurried to the front of the house to greet Bey. Just as he came into the room—wonder of wonders—the lights came back on. And Bey exclaimed, "Oh, David! You *brought the light!"* Al and Susan and Alex and David then gave Bey a mini-concert—straight from the heart of a loving God.

Just after her 103rd birthday, Bey suffered a small stroke which gradually affected her memory-store of poems and prayers and Scripture passages. She could no longer "pull them down" with the certainty and ease she had enjoyed in the past. Her movement was compromised as well. She told people she was paralyzed, though that was not precisely true. Still, it felt that way to her: that she was immobilized for the first time in her life. Caring for her became more demanding physically.

Nancy came up from Texas to visit for longer periods. Upon arrival she said to me, "Gosh! You look just like the old horse in *Gone with the Wind*. "Thanks," said I, but I knew it was true: I was wearing thin after almost ten years of eldercare duty, and welcomed my dear sister's help. We both filled in when Bey's C.N.A. was away, and at night. This meant hands-on physical help, for which neither Nancy nor I had been trained. Not surprisingly, our backs began to hurt and we both were visiting a chiropractor regularly. At one point we put Bey in a nearby skilled-nursing facility for two weeks of respite care while Nancy went home to see about her family in Texas. While she was away, I ordered a professional *lift* which would enable us to transfer Bey from place to place without doing damage to our backs.

As soon as Nancy came back we explained to Bey why we had ordered the lift, and she looked puzzled. "What I don't understand," she said, "is why everyone around here has gotten so weak." She never for a moment considered her part of the equation, and was convinced that if we would just get her up, she could move about and get the exercise she needed. So, *why weren't we doing it?* And right there in a nutshell you had the difference between Bey and Jane. Bey was a fighter, someone who was convinced she could *do it*—whatever the *it* was. People just jolly well needed to do their part, and she would do hers, without a doubt. Bey was "the little engine that *could*" from the famous children's story. She always *could*, and was ready for any challenge.

My Texas children planned to come for Christmas 2003. Knowing that Bey would be so pleased to see them, and they her, I also knew that caregivers tend to disappear over the holidays and that we would end up *being* the caregivers—all of us. By this time I was feeling "used up" and not up to organizing such a rota. Once again I made an executive decision: to have Bey in respite care over the holidays, with us visiting her daily. It seemed like a good plan, and she was given a spacious room which could accommodate all of our family visitors at once. *Great.*

Not great. We had signed up for just two weeks of respite care, and when we tried to extend it, we found that her room was already spoken for. She was moved to a very small, shared room on another hall—a totally different situation. The first time I visited her there she told me, "This is like being in a horse-stall." Christmas was coming, so I reminded her that Jesus himself had been born in a horse-stall, so maybe it wasn't such a bad place after all. Bad joke, as it turned out. She felt out of place and unhappy, and there was just nothing I could do about it. She wanted so much to be in her own home, hosting her family for Christmas as she had done so many times in the past. It was just not to be.

The Lord had a better plan: to take her to heaven where she could sing with the *real* angel chorus this Christmas. Those angels, true to form, came to *collect* her on the morning of December 17, 2003. The nurses could not wait to tell us how she had summoned them and asked—with obvious excitement—"Do you *see them?* Do you see all those *angels?* They are *everywhere!*" Of course, I wish I had been there—how could I not? I *could* have been, had I followed an urge to stop by on my way home from YMCA exercise class. Instead, knowing she was expecting me early that afternoon, I repressed the urge. Who knows? My presence might have reminded her of yet another detail in her well-planned funeral; my presence might actually have kept the angels away.

Those details had been very much on her mind during my visit the previous afternoon. First, having summoned me to the hospital, she had made that remarkable confession, "I've been wrong. I've been wrong. Please forgive me . . ." I knew immediately that she was referring to her criticism to others in the family, of a certain *"Mrs. Pulkingham"* who seemed to think she was in charge of her. Obviously the Holy Spirit had revised her opinion of me here at the eleventh hour, and in so doing had lifted a heavy burden from our entire family. The *last* thing we wanted was for her to die unhappy. So this was her last and very great gift to us. I assured her of my forgiveness, told her I was tending to all those details about the funeral that meant so much to her, that everything would be fine. I kissed her goodbye—never dreaming it would be the last time—and said, "I'll see you tomorrow."

Another touching thing about Bey's passing was this: the last two people she talked to on the morning she passed away were Savannah, her household helper, and James her gardener. She had the nurse find their phone numbers and called them to say goodbye. She told James, "Today I'm going to be with the angels." Then she added, "Take good care of my flowers . . ." Savannah and James were as much part of the fabric of her life as any of her blood kin. There was a deep bond of affection there. They had been true to her, and she to them—to the very end.

Her pastor, Craig McMahan, wrote to me afterwards: "I was the recipient of far more blessing from your precious mother than I was ever able to give to her. In all of my ministry—past, present, and future—I will never meet another person who will measure the spiritual stature of Mrs. Carr. Frederick Buechner says that saints are the handkerchiefs that God drops in his holy flirtation with the world. Our beloved "Bey" was certainly a lacey wooing graciously dropped across our path by a winking God."

> "Precious in the sight of the Lord
> is the death of his saints."
> Psalm 116: 15

TWENTY-FOUR

LIFE MOVES ON

Such a parade of departures; life will never be the same. It will actually be . . . *richer?* My priest/friend Jeff Schiffmayer brought this truth home from his experiences on the mission field in Malawi. The Africans, he said, believe that a person's spirit is more clearly known *after* that person's death than before. So I suppose people's earthly foibles and shortcomings tend to cloud our vision of who they *are* in their inmost being. After that which is earthly has passed away, spirit can speak to spirit unhampered; and this is how people we have loved continue to enrich our lives.

In the years since these dearly beloved ones left on their heavenly journey, several experiences stand out:

One was a memorable train trip to Alexandria, Virginia, in the company of three life-long Carolina friends. Meeting us there were my Carolina brother, my Texas sister and brother-in-law, one son and one daughter, as well as two friends from Celebration. I was to receive an honorary degree, *Doctor of Humane Letters,* from the Theological Seminary there. As I stood listening to the words of Bishop Peter Lee, who made the presentation, Graham's spirit was palpably present to me. What was being described was the fruit of a ministry Graham and I had shared, and shared with many, over the years. It was not about me; it was about us, and I knew it. I rejoiced that someone of stature, representing a major institution within the Episcopal

Church, was voicing recognition of this ministry, despite the clouds that had hung about since 1993. I rejoiced to be able to receive this *posthumous* honor on Graham's behalf.

Returning to Carolina on *Amtrak,* my three friends and I were nearing our destination and commenting, "What a perfect trip this has been. How absolutely delightful." The event itself, our accommodations, the fellowship enjoyed: absolutely praiseworthy in every respect. As the laudations went on, I noticed the train was slowing down noticeably. Burlington was still ten miles away, so it was puzzling that we were . . . coming . . . to . . . a . . . total . . . stop. Gazing into the pitch-blackness outside, we saw nothing but scrubby bushes and a few trees, and darkness. What is going on?

An engine failure as it turns out, and we were the fortunate ones, being just a few miles from home and able to be rescued off the train, while others heading for distant places sat and waited for a new engine to be attached. This inconvenient ending to an idyllic trip seemed to be the Lord's gentle, humorous reminder: *we're not in heaven quite yet.* In every perfect event there is bound to be a hiccup, something unforseen that turns up. We can just expect it.

In our lives as well, perfection is beyond reach. We are pilgrims on a journey, growing in the compassion of Jesus, learning to forgive one another's flaws—since we all have them. We hear the poet's words to

> *Ring the bells that still can ring. Forget your perfect offering. There is a crack in everything. That's how the light gets in.*
>
> From *Anthem* by Leonard Cohen

These earthen vessels, so fragile, so beautiful, are where God has chosen to place the Kingdom's treasure. Gazing through glass at my newborn grand-twins in the N.I.C.U. unit of a Texas hospital, I am seeing one of the Lord's little miracles before my very eyes. Beyond the obvious delight of becoming a grandmother again at age eighty, there is this fresh sense of wonder. God has great surprises around every corner, it seems. One of the most delightful surprises has been Celebration's new chapel in the heart of Aliquippa, rising like a *Phoenix* from the desolation around it. Truly our God can create beauty out of ashes, beauty where there had been only grim reminders of the past. Each year I look forward to returning there as a Companion of the Community, to worship with my friends at Celebration. Meanwhile, the twins, with their teeming three-year-old energy and their happy songs remind me afresh of the divine creativity. They cause me to reflect on our beginnings and endings:

The seasons of the year have much to teach us about the seasons of life. There are spring-times of tender new growth, summers of ripeness and maturity, autumn's richness of color even as energies fade, and winter's willingness to let it all die in order that new beauty may unfold in God's time. My return to North Carolina was a return to these four seasons. In all my travels around the globe, I have never known such perfectly fashioned, balanced seasons as are the four we have here in the old North state. I marvel at each in its course. Each puts me in touch with certain undeniable truths about my own life.

The first is that I had a remarkable springtime, to have been nurtured by Bey and Leo. What a parentage, what a legacy: I had no inkling just how lucky I was—though I prefer to see it through the lens of blessedness. How *blessed* I was to have been born of this union of God-loving, God-fearing parents. Only years later, when I had known many born into strife-ridden, abusive families and sent on their life journey bearing wounds of that strife: only then did I realize how blessed I had been in my birthing, in my upbringing.

The summering of my life had all to do with varieties of fruit-bearing. Because of a wonderful man to whom I said "I do" in my early twenties, linking my life with his, I have known the blessing of bearing six beautiful children who have now reached maturity themselves. My life has also borne musical fruit, there again not on my own, but as the spiritual harvest of a richly shared life in Christ. My friends at Redeemer Church and in the Community of Celebration were the catalyst and oftimes the laboratory for testing this music. They were part of the plant that produced the fruit. No plant, no fruit.

My autumn years have been aglow with color—some of it purple-hued with sorrow, some of it burning red with new zeal, some of it golden with the mellowness that seems to come with age. It is easier now to see the meaning of things than when I was dashing through them. It is easier now to let go of things, and of people. The *things* have less grip on my soul; the *people* I can just enjoy for who they are. This includes my children, whom I no longer need to *bring up*, and my grandchildren, whom I never did. What joy.

Now winter comes. What will winter bring? Harsh gales blowing strong against an aging frame? Very likely. We are more vulnerable as we grow older. Bodies tend to wear out—some sooner than others. At the moment I am a hermit on a hill, something of a lone ranger again, yet far from being *really* alone. My life is fed by rich memories and unbidden dreams, sustained by faithful friends close at hand as well as many scattered around the globe, and enriched by a family who loves me. I am surrounded by many creatures who also consider this place their home: young squirrels and rabbits who dash across the driveway—they know I won't hit them—as I drive in. *Welcome home,* they say. The birds *sing* their message. On the first day of December I notice a red rosebud outside on a bush I had watched all season in hopes of a rose. Finally, just two days before heavy frost, the flower has come. *Never give up on late bloomers,* the Lord reminds me. I pluck the rose and bring it in out of the cold, place it in a tiny vase where it can smile at me. Simple pleasures. Much later I ask myself, "Was that rose sent to remind me there is more late blooming for *me* to do?"

If I should die tonight—let the record show—my life has been abundantly blessed. The Lord is my Shepherd, and I have lacked nothing. If I should live longer days—let the record also show—my one desire is to love and serve the Lord all the days of my life.

Taste and see that the Lord is good;
happy are they who trust in him!
Psalm 34: 8